WITS UNIVERSITY AT
100

From Excavation to Innovation

Contents

Foreword by Judy Dlamini vi
Introduction: Looking Back, Moving Forward 1

Chapter 1: Origins 11

The Last Word: Benedict Vilakazi 33
    Wits Pioneer: Johnny Clegg 37
Dynamite Underground: Wits Geosciences 41
Fighting the Good Fight 47
    Wits Pioneer: Stephen Matseoane 52
Life as We Know It: The Story of Life 55
    Wits Pioneer: Advocate Thuli Madonsela 62

Chapter 2: Space and Place 67

Behind the Scenes of #FeesMustFall 85
    Activists, Scientists and a Lifetime of Service: Maurice Smithers 90
Wits Rural Campus: The Hidden Gem 93
Knowing Your Place 99
    Activists, Scientists and a Lifetime of Service: Patrick Soon-Shiong and Michele B. Chan 106
Leading the Charge 111
    Activists, Scientists and a Lifetime of Service: Bhekokuzakuye 'Keith' Mdlalose 118

Chapter 3: The Future 125

Light Years Ahead: Invention, Innovation and the Structured Light Lab 139
Minding the Matter 145
    Wits Futurists Lead the Way: Achille Mbembe 150
Fringe of the Future 153
    Wits Futurists Lead the Way: Marcus Byrne 160
African Art Beat: Wits Art Museum 167
    I Have a Dream ... 172

Chapter 4: The Next Century Begins Now 179

Afterword by Zeblon Vilakazi 188
Acknowledgements 191
Timeline 192
Notes 205
Interviewees 208
Bibliography and Source Material 210
Index 211

FOREWORD

The University of the Witwatersrand, Johannesburg, known colloquially as Wits University, is a national treasure that has advanced society for over 100 years. It is renowned for its academic and research excellence, its innovation, social leadership and commitment to justice, enquiry and the search for truth.

Wits has evolved over the last 100 years, rooted in its place and space in Johannesburg, but impacting globally. Its origins and its trajectory – shaped by the staff, students and alumni who have walked its corridors and are charting its future potential – are captured in moments throughout this book. We also explore some of the challenges that Wits has had to endure during this time.

The birthplace of new ideas, Wits developed with the City of Johannesburg, and its roots are inextricably linked to that of industry and mining. Since the early 1900s, Wits has developed the high-level scarce skills required in adequate measure to move Johannesburg and the South African economy forward. For example, Wits' journey with the mining industry, from excavation to innovation, has evolved over the decades. The University is now working with the mining industry to digitise mines, to make mining safer, to transform its workforce, gender profile and leadership, and to ensure that it is environmentally sustainable.

This University has nurtured over 200 000 formidable alumni over ten decades, many of whom have made their mark in Africa and across the globe. These are creators and artists, inventors and innovators, thinkers and intellectuals, problem-posers and problem-solvers, change-makers and social leaders who serve as catalysts for change in a rapidly moving world.

These are Witsies who are curious about the world, who seek new knowledge, think critically and are enthusiastic about changing the world for good. Some of the famous names associated with Wits include Nelson Mandela, Robert Sobukwe, Aaron Klug, Sydney Brenner, Benedict Vilakazi, Sibongile Khumalo, Nadine Gordimer, Thuli Madonsela, Johnny Clegg, Hugh Masekela, Adrian Gore, Phillip Tobias, George Bizos, Koos Becker, Dikgang Moseneke, Joe Veriava, Jody Kollapen, Sir David King, Bruce Fordyce, Ivan Glasenberg, Gary Bailey, Ahmed Kathrada, Joel Joffe, and Precious and Patrice Motsepe – some of whom feature in this book.

Wits is driven by curiosity that spurs innovation and many spectacular discoveries and world-firsts have emanated from this great institution. From the Taung Child and Little Foot to *Homo naledi*, the many discoveries related to the origins of plants, animals, hominids and the thousands of archaeological artefacts that help to tell the story of humans are unprecedented.

Having produced many world-firsts, Wits is a global innovator. For example, the first radar set was developed at Wits within three months of the outbreak of the Second World War. In the very same place where it tested successfully – outside the Great Hall – a team is currently testing another world-first: the secure transmission of data through light. Wits was the first African university to own an IBM mainframe computer. Today, it is the first African university to have access to a quantum computer, which will undoubtedly transform our lives in the future.

A social leader, Wits was born out of protest in the early 1900s, and its official opening was postponed by about six months due to strikes and the Rand Revolt. The first protest against fee increases took place in the 1930s, and intermittently thereafter, escalating over time and culminating in the #FeesMustFall protests. Protests against the apartheid regime spanned several decades, often resulting in the University being heavily penalised by the state. Some Wits activists paid the ultimate price in their fight for freedom.

Today, Wits has taken a strong stance against gender-based harm and launched several initiatives to address gender inequality in the academy, in the workplace and in society. Wits is one of the founding champions of the United Nations Women's HeForShe movement, which is part of the IMPACT 10x10x10 initiative to unveil ground-breaking solutions that have the potential to see gender equality achieved in our lifetime. Using an intersectional lens to address gender and racial inequality in academia gave birth to the Female Academic Leaders Fellowship, a centenary initiative that seeks to address the representation of women, and especially black women, in leadership in academia. Wits is tackling inequality in one of the most unequal countries in the world, an issue that, together with climate change and sustainability, is a priority for the University as it looks towards its next century.

Wits impacts beyond its sphere of influence geographically, intellectually and socially. The University is based on the ridge of the Witwatersrand, which I am told is what gives it the edge. Its footprint extends way beyond its lecture theatres and research laboratories, as is demonstrated in the 'Space and Place' chapter of this book. Wits hosts South Africa's only privately funded teaching hospital, the Wits Donald Gordon Medical Centre, which develops hundreds of specialists annually. The world's first living donor liver transplant from an HIV-positive mother to her HIV-negative child took place in 2017. Wits also owns caves and land rich in fossils in the Cradle of Humankind World Heritage Site where staff and students explore, discover and conduct research. In Mpumalanga, the Wits Rural Campus conducts world-class longitudinal research, while back in Braamfontein, the Tshimologong Digital Innovation Precinct brings people together to engage in digital entrepreneurial and innovation activities that transform our world for good.

Wits is home to two commercial companies; a Planetarium that will soon be transformed into the Wits Digital Dome; the Wits Art Museum, which houses over 9 000 works of unique African art; the Origins Centre; the Palaeosciences Centre and Fossil Vault, which houses invaluable fossils, and the Historical Papers Research Archive, which curates national treasures such as former president

Nelson Mandela's Rivonia Trial papers, on behalf of the people of the world.

But Wits could not exist without the people who have made this university great – the staff, joint staff, students, alumni, donors and friends of Wits across the world who continue to make a difference in their sphere of influence every day. Some of them are profiled in this book. They are the ones who stand up for social justice and pursue the truth. They have a passion for progress, empower others and change the world for the better. These are the people, like you, who stand up and stand out, not for themselves, but for others, to secure our collective futures.

I hope that you will learn more about Wits through the stories of the people reflected on these pages and that you, too, will be inspired to change our world. May we achieve equality in our lifetime, working together, for good.

Dr Judy Dlamini

Chancellor of the University of the Witwatersrand, Johannesburg

Photo: Shivan Parusnath

Wits Central Block as photographed in 1929 (left) combined with an image of the Wits Great Hall taken in 2000 (right). Photo: (left) Dr Martinus de Kock and (right) Shivan Parusnath

INTRODUCTION: LOOKING BACK, MOVING FORWARD

A century. One hundred not out. A significant milestone for Wits University. Add to that the fact that Wits was founded and has grown and thrived in a city not much given to looking back. Johannesburg, the City of Gold, has an edgy urban history befitting a place that began life as a mining town, and its development, like that of Wits, is inextricably linked to mining and political and civic activism.

This book presents a narrative of Wits as a living and dynamic institution, celebrating its existence through its people, many of whom, in one way or another, have positively impacted on the world. Their stories – some of them told in their own words – map the University's current and future vision, and show how Wits has transitioned from colonial, racialised and historical inequality to a global symbol of a flourishing and inclusive society.

There are many stories to tell, too many for one publication, and this book holds but a sample from the broad array on offer. Three major themes run through the text – origins, space and place, and the imagined future – accompanied by appropriate stories, photographs and illustrations. These stories have been chosen to reflect the diversity of the protagonists, the subject matter, and historical periods, and their contribution to the public good.

INTRODUCTION

ORIGINS

These are stories that explore Wits' beginnings and early years, but they are not here for nostalgia's sake. Institutional memory gives life to a place and provides a compelling way of understanding how far we as a people, a city, a country and an institution have come. Memories provide perspective on current concerns. Invariably, they also provide hope for an imagined future. In this section, we look to people who have memories of Wits' early years to explore what life was like back then; to understand the role that Wits played in shaping South Africa through its teaching, research and scientific endeavours; to uncover how Wits shaped society through the arts; and to appreciate how the University is embedded in Africa's cultural fabric.

Present-day aerial drone image of Wits University and greater Johannesburg shows how the University has expanded over time and across the City. Photo: Shivan Parusnath

In May 1957, a march was organised by Wits students and academics against the Separate Universities Bill. Source: University of the Witwatersrand's Central Records Office and Archives

SPACE AND PLACE

Wits occupies a central place in Johannesburg and its history is inextricably intertwined with that of the City in fundamental ways. The University is edgy, urban(e) and entrenched in the economic heartland of the continent. Wits both 'makes' history – it has produced many of Johannesburg's social, economic, academic and political leaders – and recreates history, through its study of the history and archaeology of the region. We have captured these stories of place through narratives of space, politics, urban geography and inclusivity/exclusivity.

INNOVATION AND AN IMAGINED FUTURE

These are stories of the imagination, which have not yet been realised or which are in the process of being realised. They include inspiring narratives around digital transformation and culture, society, and technology like artificial intelligence, online and machine learning, and big data, which have immense potential for changing and improving lives.

VISION AND VALUES

The trajectory that marks the achievement of Wits to this point, in the year 2022, where it is a globally ranked, powerful African university, is not just a tale of triumph and achievement. Human frailty, unforeseen setbacks, obstacles and failure need to be factored into any journey of progression over a hundred years. The constantly changing context of the time – political, social and economic – has presented Wits with many challenges along the way. These have been internal and external, and have demanded ongoing self-reflection, re-evaluation and an honest scrutiny of value systems in a changing world.

Wits' values have remained relevant and steadfast throughout its history. They are reflected in the manner in which Wits conducts its business, but they are also embedded in the three themes chosen for this celebratory book. Integrally linked to the themes, and expressed below as statements of intent, is Wits' vision, as espoused in the past and just as relevant for the future of the University.

We lead change. Wits is renowned for its world-class research and academic excellence. Prominent in these efforts have been its commitment to social justice and the advancement of the public good. Tied to its anti-racism and non-discrimination position is the University's insistence on institutional autonomy. The ability to lead change extends to the many innovations and world-firsts achieved by Wits staff, students and alumni over the years. Wits remains a premier university on the continent and continues to lead from the front. From the ways in which Wits responded with resistance to state crackdowns and legislation during the apartheid era to how

INTRODUCTION

it has shaped contemporary thinking about decolonising education, from investing in the first IBM mainframe to hosting the first IBM quantum computing initiative, from developing radar to developing digital mines, Wits always leads change.

We harness the power of place. Wits is intimately embedded in Johannesburg, eGoli, the City of Gold. Much of the history of the institution is tied to the parallel development of the City, which grew out of a gold-mining camp. Wits started as a college to cater for the hugely influential mining industry that cropped up on the Witwatersrand. Witsies have been instrumental in changing the face of Johannesburg and, indeed, the region and the country. Stories in this thread include how Wits' research has contributed to the architecture of Johannesburg and the Gauteng City-Region, and has positively impacted on society through its food security, climate change and sustainability endeavours, for example.

We create and apply knowledge. Through a focus on Wits alumni and academics in a wider national purview, this section focuses on stories that demonstrate how Wits has shaped the country's psyche. These stories include Wits' groundbreaking work in law, anthropology and palaeoanthropology, and its pioneering work in digital transformation, electrical engineering and the Internet of Things.

We are global. Wits has an international sphere of influence. Wits Vice-Chancellor and Principal Zeblon Vilakazi affirms that Wits has the ability to compete and lead from the Global South. Stories in this section range from Wits' role in helping to shape post-colonial thinking about Africa to the global impact of Wits' vaccine research in the fight against the coronavirus.

HOW TO READ THIS BOOK
Wits University at 100: From Excavation to Innovation is not simply a history or an archive of the first hundred years of Wits, but rather a series of snapshots – of people, events, places and ideas – that demonstrate how the University came to be a cutting-edge institution and how it plans to continue this tradition for the next century.

You can read the book in conventional fashion, from beginning to end, or you can choose to dip in and out, using the thematic colour code and chapter titles as a guide, depending on your interest.

The 100-year timeline of key events, historical moments and defining issues is intended to be a helpful reference marker to bookend each of the ten decades making up the centenary. It should provide an understanding of the sweep of time both on the world stage and from the perspective of the Global South.

Some of the information in the chapters will, of necessity, overlap as the three themes of origins, space and place, and the imagined future pertain to a particular discipline, time period or the individuals who shared their stories. If you are intrigued by the historical aspects of how the University came to be in Johannesburg in the early 1920s, and by the economic imperatives that gave the institution its early identity and funding, then read chapter 1, 'Origins'.

LOOKING BACK, MOVING FORWARD

The main campus of Wits University in the 1950s consisted of a few buildings centred around the Great Hall. Note the mine dumps and cooling towers in close vicinity. Source: University of the Witwatersrand's Central Records Office and Archives

The Centre for Applied Legal Studies (CALS) is a human rights organisation based in the Wits School of Law. The organisation combines research, advocacy and litigation in order to connect academia and social justice. Photo: Shivan Parusnath

INTRODUCTION

If you wish to trace the voice of Wits as an open university, evidenced by its independent intellectual thought, academic excellence and opposition to all forms of state repression, read chapter 2, 'Space and Place'. This section also demonstrates the reach of the University and its influence in Johannesburg and further afield, both geographically and intellectually.

Chapter 3, 'The Future', explores Wits' leadership in a world that is constantly evolving. It creates and enables an environment that fosters and celebrates creativity on every possible and improbable level, and leaves you with no doubt that this world-class institution will continue to make its mark for the next 100 years.

The final chapter, 'The Next Century Begins Now', reaffirms Wits' commitment to its values and its responsibilities, confirmed through the words of Wits' Vice-Chancellor and Principal, Professor Zeblon Vilakazi: 'Our centennial year offers us an opportunity to build on the successes of our past, to value our current work, and to shape tomorrow. There are three core areas that we will maintain as Wits transitions into its next century: developing excellent graduates who leave their mark on society; conducting world-class research and fostering innovation; and using our location in the economic heartland of Africa to lead from the Global South.'[1]

Robert F Kennedy's historic speech at Wits as part of his 'A Ripple of Hope' visit to the country in 1966 was inspirational. Source: University of the Witwatersrand's Central Records Office and Archives

The steps at the entrance of the Oppenheimer Life Sciences Building display Wits' 'For Good' manifesto. Photo: Daniel Born

LOOKING BACK, MOVING FORWARD

Wits University Central Block in 1937
Source: University of the Witwatersrand's Central Records Office and Archives

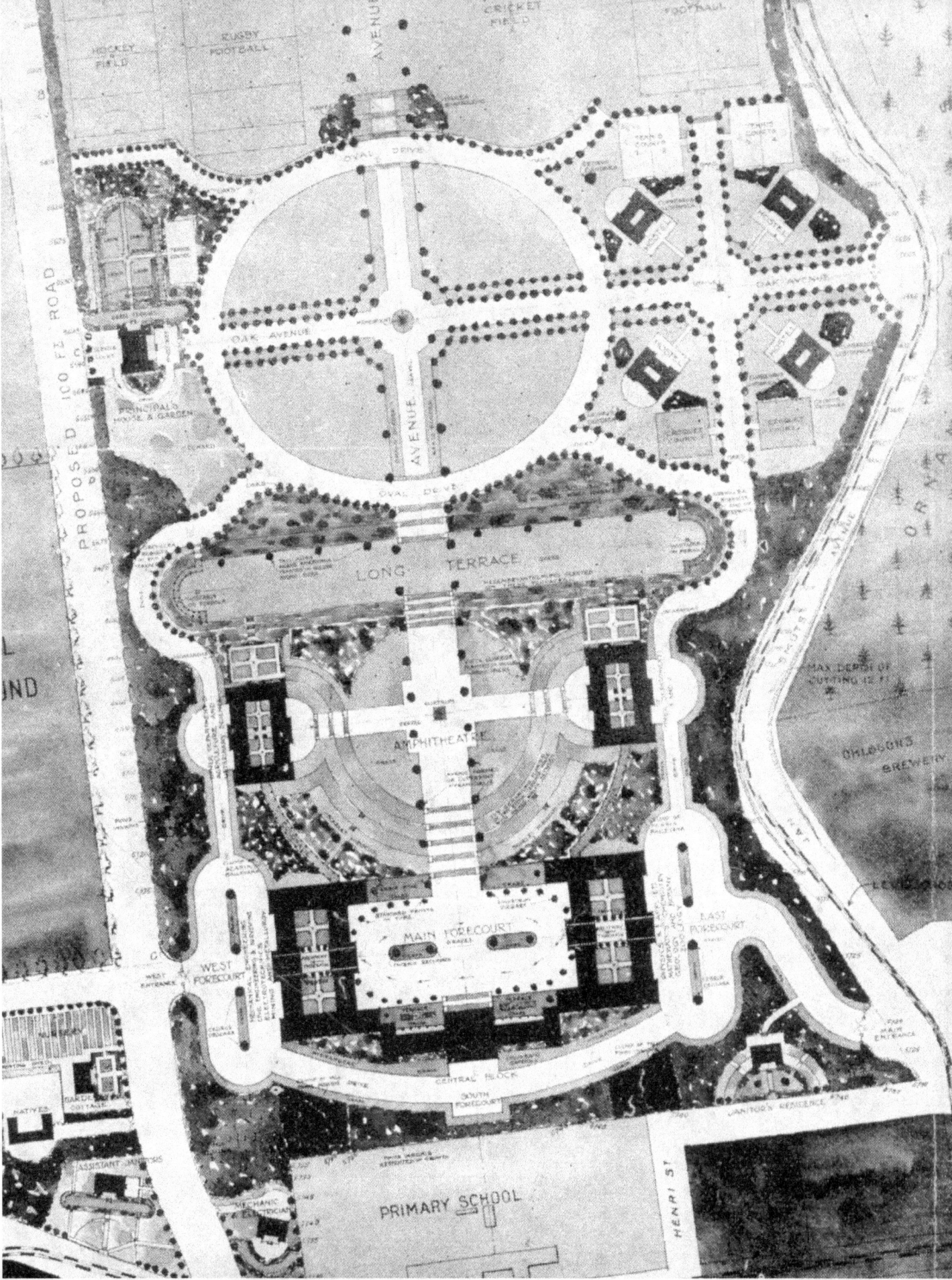

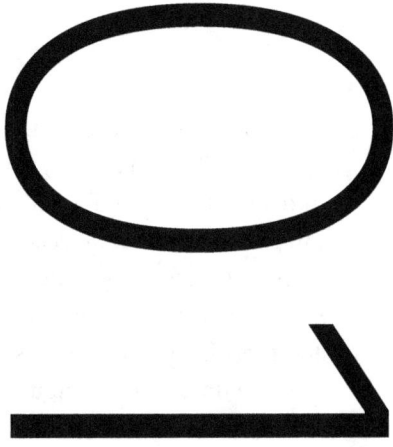

Origins

OVERVIEW

The origins and subsequent growth of Wits University are inseparable from the development of the mining industry through the twentieth century and the expansion of Johannesburg through the same period. Their intertwined histories are evident in how the University and City grew spatially and architecturally.

The links between the birth of Wits and the development of the City are shown in Wits' character as an institution of higher learning; the nature of the people who were influential in its development; the diverse academic disciplines, thoughts and ideologies; and the effect on multiple levels of society. The University's development as a crucial place in Johannesburg, part of its fabric, has been an organic one, allowing the people of Wits – its staff, students and communities – to develop, breathe and negotiate their way creatively.

Wits has always thrived on the energy and innovation of the industrial heartland of South Africa. From the very beginning, the site of the University campus was rooted in the spatial identity of the City of Johannesburg, with emerging skyscrapers in the old central business district and nascent mine dumps serving as backdrops.

A hundred years after its inauguration on 4 October 1922, an aerial view of Wits as it stands in the City today will testify to the institution's integration and urban reach. The University is spread across five academic campuses in Braamfontein and Parktown, Sturrock Park, and the Wits Rural Campus in Mpumalanga. The Braamfontein Campus East is the traditional home of the humanities and some science faculties, and houses the administrative seat of the University. Across the M1 highway lies Braamfontein Campus West, the former home of the old Rand Show. The Braamfontein campuses are bordered by Empire Road on the north, Jan Smuts Avenue on the east, Jorissen Street and Enoch Sontonga Avenue on the south and Annet Road on the west.

The Braamfontein Campus West was originally the Milner Park showgrounds, acquired by the University in 1984 from the Witwatersrand Agricultural Society. It features the architecturally significant Tower of Light, built for the Empire Exhibition in 1936. The tower has been retained and serves as a landmark of the redeveloped Braamfontein Campus West, which houses the Faculty of Engineering and the Built Environment, and the Faculty of Commerce, Law and Management, amongst other entities.

Wits has three academic campuses in the suburb of Parktown. The Wits Education Campus (WEC) houses the School of Education, within the Faculty of Humanities. East of the WEC (across York Road) lies the Wits Faculty of Health Sciences, which adjoins the Charlotte Maxeke Johannesburg Academic Hospital, built in 1979. The Phillip V Tobias Building on the Princess of Wales Terrace was opened in 2014. To the west of the WEC (across Victoria Avenue) lies the Wits Management Campus, which houses two postgraduate schools – the iconic Wits Business School and the Wits School of Governance.

GOLD RUNS THROUGH IT

As much as Wits seems part of the cityscape today, the University had its genesis in 1896 in the diamond-mining town of Kimberley, in the Northern Cape. Johannesburg was for a long time readily identifiable by the gold-coloured mine dumps on the City's margins, but in its infancy the City was by no means the African city that it is today. It started its economic life as a rough tented mining camp, filled with fortune-hunting prospectors from all over the world lured to the Reef by the promise of gold-bearing rock beneath the ground. Some struck it rich, while others fell by the wayside.

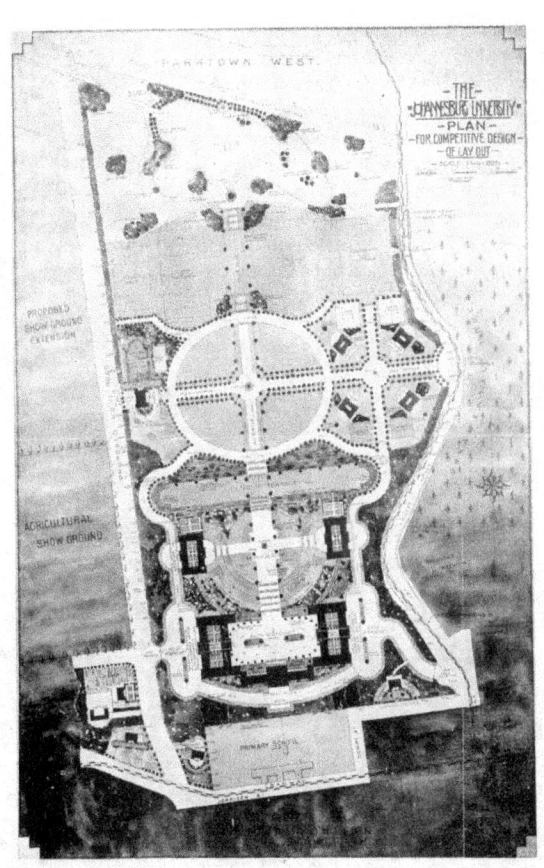

A proposal for the East Campus extension by architect Harold Porter, 1919. The design of J. Lyon & War Fallon won the 'lay-out competition'; Porter's design came second. Source: University of the Witwatersrand's Central Records Office and Archives

ORIGINS

Early collaboration between higher education and industry. On 10 August 1896, the first five students enrolled for the third year of the mining course at the School of Mines in Kimberley. All five students passed and moved to Johannesburg, where, through the Chamber of Mines, they were committed to the care of various mine managers on the Rand. Source: University of the Witwatersrand's Central Records Office and Archives

In 1920, the South African School of Mines and Technology became, by an Act of Parliament, the University College, Johannesburg. Source: University of the Witwatersrand's Central Records Office and Archives

The inauguration of Wits staff and students of 1907. Source: University of the Witwatersrand's Central Records Office and Archives

It was not long before the mining companies took hold. The influence of the mining magnates, known collectively as the Randlords, on the public life of Johannesburg at the beginning of the twentieth century is undeniable. Many Johannesburg institutions and the shaping of the City itself were influenced by the economic decisions taken by the mining companies.

It was through the agency of the mining company owners that the School of Mines, originally established in 1896 in Kimberley, was transferred to the new fields on the Reef in 1904, a move that unknowingly gave birth to what would become the University of the Witwatersrand. You could therefore say that, technically, Wits is 118 years old!

By 1904 Johannesburg was already the economic hub of the country. The school was renamed the Transvaal Technical Institute, with premises on Eloff Street. Other departments in broader arts and science disciplines were added, and in 1906 it was renamed the Transvaal University College. In 1910 the Transvaal government created a separate campus for the college in Pretoria – providing, in part, the groundwork for what would in time become the University of Pretoria. The institution in Johannesburg was renamed the South African School of Mines and Technology, using the former Trade Union Congress Building on Plein Square as its headquarters.

THE INAUGURATION (AND PROTESTS)
In 1917 the school began to provide teaching space for broader arts and science courses, making it a university college in all but name. In 1920, it was named the University College, Johannesburg, and full university status was granted in 1922.

The official inauguration was set for 1 March of that year, but the Rand Rebellion and other events saw the ceremony moved to 4 October. The inauguration, and also the first graduation, took place in the City Hall in Rissik Street. Presiding over the inauguration was Prince Arthur of Connaught, governor-general of the Union of South Africa. He became the University's first chancellor and Professor Jan H Hofmeyr its first principal.

Achieving official university status was not plain sailing but was met with protests. There were many influential figures at the time who opposed the idea of a university in the city, including Cecil John Rhodes. It was widely considered, among the wealthy capitalist classes, that Johannesburg in the early twentieth century was no place for an institution of higher learning, considering its genesis as a freewheeling mining town. Many deemed it to be too 'rough and ready' to offer a conducive environment for serious study. In 1926, Hofmeyr described the City in these words: 'We have this twentieth century City of Johannesburg with the ethic of the mining camp still sometimes revealing itself – all too painfully.'[2]

THE 1922 MINERS' STRIKE
In the same year that the University was inaugurated, miners' strikes were emerging, and the traditions of social leadership and protest have since been associated with Wits. The so-called Red Revolt across Johannesburg and the Reef was inspired by the entrenched racist labour practices on the mines that guaranteed semi-skilled white workers certain jobs. Mine owners, concerned about a fall in the gold price, proposed to employ Black workers in these positions to cut labour costs, causing a racially inflected 'Bolshevik' uprising of whites-only workers and communist political parties. What began as a general labour strike quickly became an armed insurrection.

On 10 March 1922, the then prime minister General Jan Smuts, proclaimed martial law. Seeking to quell the revolt, he came to Johannesburg to personally direct operations against the white mine workers. The strikers fought across the East Rand of the Reef, briefly occupying Benoni, Springs and Brakpan. In Johannesburg, they entrenched themselves in Fordsburg and along the Brixton Ridge to the west of Milner Park. Smuts, who cracked down on the insurrection with the full force of the army, used the Wits Biology Block, which

Black miners were hired to cut labour costs, as mine owners were concerned about a fall in the gold price. Source: University of the Witwatersrand's Central Records Office and Archives

A view of the crowd that gathered for the Wits inauguration ceremony on 4 October 1922, when HRH Prince Arthur of Connaught laid the foundation stones for Central Block. Source: University of the Witwatersrand's Central Records Office and Archives

was nearing completion, to survey and plan an attack on Cottesloe School and the Ridge. A contemporary map noted that on 12 March 1922, 'Brixton Ridge was captured, aeroplanes and guns cooperating with infantry, and the first severe blow dealt against revolutionaries in Johannesburg'.[3] The fighting along the Rand lasted four days, with 153 people killed and many more injured before the strike was finally subdued. As many as 2 200 strikers were taken prisoner and four were executed.

Wits' close ties with the mining industry were a factor in drawing the battle lines for the University and where the University's sympathies lay in this conflict was never in question. The strikers were perceived as hated 'Bolsheviks'. Staff and students alike, many of them veterans of the First World War and loyal to Smuts, rallied to his defence, with a good number enlisting in the army or volunteering as special constables to patrol Johannesburg's streets in the aftermath.

THE RANDLORDS

While neither Wits nor Johannesburg itself would have come into being were it not for gold and the industry it spawned, it was not always a harmonious relationship. Given their importance in the mining companies, it is somewhat surprising that the Randlords didn't exert a more direct influence over the origins and development of Wits, given that many of their fortunes were intertwined with the City. The major growth of the University happened a little later in the twentieth century.

In 1925, the Prince of Wales officially opened the Central Block (now the Robert Sobukwe Block) in its current location. The building's grand neo-classical façade was for many years

Jan H Hofmeyr (right) was appointed principal of the South African School of Mines and Technology at the age of 24, in 1919. He and General Jan Smuts (left) attended the inauguration ceremony in 1922. Source: University of the Witwatersrand's Central Records Office and Archives

The Randlord-era mansion Savernake was built in 1904 and later bequeathed to the University as the estate of the late Dr Bernard Price, former resident director of the Victoria Falls and Transvaal Power Company (now the state-owned entity Eskom). Source: University of the Witwatersrand's Central Records Office and Archives

just that – a façade. Financial shortfalls meant that the temporary wood and iron buildings that were there since its inception were only finally replaced in 1940, but not before a huge fire in 1931 destroyed much of the building. The blaze, tragically, destroyed the irreplaceable Gubbins collection of Africana. John Gubbins (1877–1935), a Cambridge-educated historian and minor mining magnate, had placed his extensive collection with the University for safekeeping. The 1931 fire also consumed the Philip Papers, the collection of the letters of eighteenth-century missionary and activist John Philip. A more permanent – and safer – library building, what is today the William Cullen Library, was erected the following year.

Sir Lionel Phillips, who was briefly exiled for his role in Cecil John Rhodes' Jameson Raid, was the president of the Chamber of Mines and lived in Johannesburg for 12 years. Phillips revived the Witwatersrand Agricultural Society that played a vital role in Wits' spatial development in the 1980s. He was also a founding trustee of the Johannesburg Art Gallery. He contributed seven significant paintings and a Rodin sculpture to the gallery. His wife, Lady Florence, was responsible for the renowned Foundation Collection. She brought in Sir Hugh Lane, a noted Irish gentleman curator, to put this collection together in order to give the City some 'European sophistication'. Lane did the same for the City Gallery in Dublin, which today bears his name.

One of the Randlord-era mansions to retain a contemporary Wits connection is Savernake in Parktown. Built in 1904, Savernake was purchased by a pioneering engineer,

ORIGINS

Dr Bernard Price, in 1913. The house was bequeathed to the University in Price's will and has served as the official residence of the vice-chancellor and principal since 1948. A long-time benefactor of the University, Price established the Bernard Price Institute for Geophysical Research and the Bernard Price Institute for Palaeontological Research at Wits. A building on the Braamfontein Campus East, which is home to the Evolutionary Studies Institute, now bears his name. The South African Institute of Electrical Engineers founded the annual Bernard Price Memorial Lecture in his honour, which is co-hosted by Wits and delivered by eminent scientists or engineers from around the world.

Jubilant graduates pose in front of the iconic Great Hall in 2020. Graduation ceremonies are dignified occasions that begin with the academic procession (chancellor, president of Wits Convocation, chairperson of Wits Council, vice-chancellor and principal, deputy vice-chancellors, guest speaker, honorary graduands, SRC president and academic staff) led by the bearer of the University mace and accompanied by the processional song, 'Ihele'. Photo: Shivan Parusnath

AN INDEPENDENT INSTITUTION

Wits was founded as an open university with a policy of non-discrimination. Hofmeyr set the tone of the University's subsequent opposition to apartheid when, during his inaugural address on 4 October 1922, while discussing the nature of a university and its desired function in a democracy, he declared that universities 'should know no distinctions of class, wealth, race or creed'.[4]

At this point, Hofmeyr was regarded as one of the country's foremost intellectuals and university administrators. A young, Oxford-educated prodigy, he was a long-term ally and confidant of Jan Smuts, for whom he would fill in as South Africa's wartime prime minister during the Second World War, while Smuts was on active duty. Hofmeyr was conciliatory and liberal in his disposition and politics, especially concerning race relations, as his stint in Smuts' cabinet during the war would prove. He explicitly opposed nascent apartheid currents within Smuts' wartime government from politicians such as JBM Hertzog and DF Malan, figures who would go on to be influential members of the National Party. Hofmeyr's liberal convictions at that point were the same as those that he had established early in his leadership of the University, providing the young institution with its abiding system of beliefs and values, many of which are continued by its current leadership and academics.

The 'colour bar', as it came to be known, reserving certain better-paid and more skilled jobs for whites in the mining industry, remained in place long after the 1922 insurrection. Although the first Black person enrolled at Wits in 1935, the advent of apartheid from 1948 curbed the intake of people of colour at the institution. The first Black mining engineer, Yusuf Sikander Joosub, registered at Wits in 1978, and graduated in 1981. It was only in 1988 that the colour bar was officially lifted for both the mining industry and universities in South Africa. With regard to mining engineering, Wits' first female mining engineer, Dale Pearson, graduated in 1994, and Wits' first Black female mining engineer, Celiwe Mosoane, in 2002.

BRICK BY BRICK

It was the South African High Commissioner, Lord Alfred Milner (who also gave his name to Milner Park, where Wits' Braamfontein Campus West stands today), who had prioritised the recommissioning of the deep-level gold mines on the Reef after the South African War (1899–1902). His efforts to establish a centre for technical mining training for artisans focused on white engineers and artisans, which was common practice for educational and professional institutions at the time, signalling the extent to which, from the beginning, Wits would be embroiled in contestation around racial discrimination and oppression.

Of course, the sprawling Wits campus of today was born from humble beginnings, and built brick by brick. From 1923, the University gradually began vacating its premises in Eloff Street to move to the first completed teaching buildings in Milner Park, on a site donated by the Johannesburg municipality. At this stage, the University had six faculties (Arts, Science, Medicine, Engineering, Law, and Commerce),

37 departments, 73 members of academic staff and around 1 000 students.

During the period between the two world wars, severe financial restrictions were imposed upon the University. Nevertheless, student numbers remained impressive – in 1939 student enrolment totalled 2 544, a number that grew to 3 100 by 1945. A sudden increase in student enrolment after the Second World War led to accommodation challenges, which were temporarily resolved by the construction of wood and galvanised-iron hutments in the centre of the campus. These huts remained in use, surprisingly, until 1972.

Between 1947 and the 1980s, the University experienced considerable growth and student numbers increased steadily. In 1963 there were 6 275 students, in 1975 admissions reached 10 600 and ten years later enrolments totalled 16 400. By 1999, Wits was home to about 20 000 students. Today, Wits has close to 40 000 registered students. The University's identity has been richly enhanced by its many students and staff from other provinces, the rest of Africa and the world, who bring with them diverse views and ideologies.

EXPANSION

As Wits grew, the acquisition of additional property became urgent. The medical library and the administrative offices of the Faculty of Health Sciences moved to a new building in Esselen Street, Hillbrow, in 1964. The Graduate School of Business Administration was established in 1968 and the Ernest

Oppenheimer Hall of Residence was formally opened in 1969 in Parktown. In the same year, the clinical departments in the new Medical School were opened. The Medical School has since moved premises and is now based in the Faculty of Health Sciences, situated in York Road, Parktown. The campus was opened on 30 August 1982. The Health Sciences administration was relocated to the Phillip V Tobias Building in 2014.

The 1970s saw the construction of the Jubilee Hall of Residence and the Wartenweiler Library on the Braamfontein Campus East, as well as the opening of the Tandem Accelerator (the first, and to date only, nuclear facility at a South African university).

Expansion into Braamfontein also took place. In 1976, Lawson's Corner (since renamed University Corner) was acquired. Senate House, the University's main administrative building, was completed in 1976 and opened in 1977. It has since been renamed Solomon Mahlangu House on request from #FeesMustFall activists in 2015/16. The Wedge, a building formerly owned by the National Institute of Metallurgy, was acquired by the University in 1979. Initially, it became the studios of the University's Department of Fine Arts but it is today the site of the renowned Origins Centre, an African anthropological and rock art museum. In 1989, the Chamber of Mines Building for the Faculty of Engineering was opened, and the brick-paved AMIC deck was built across the M1 motorway to link the East and West campuses. The renaming of the AMIC deck to the Sibanye-Stillwater Infinity Bridge was approved in 2021.

EXPANSION OUTSIDE JOHANNESBURG
The University's interests were not confined to the development and expansion of Milner Park and adjacent areas. In the 1960s, Wits acquired Sterkfontein farm, with its world-famous limestone caves rich in archaeological material, from the Stegmann family. In 1968, the neighbouring farm, Swartkrans, also a source of archaeological material, was purchased. In the same year, the University acquired excavation rights in caves of archaeological and palaeontological importance at Makapansgat in Limpopo province. Both sites are rich in the fossil remains of early hominids. In 1999, the area was declared a World Heritage Site by UNESCO as the Cradle of Humankind. As a World Heritage Site, responsibility for the site shifted from the University to the Gauteng provincial government, which has developed the site into a world-class tourist attraction and is responsible for its protection.

The University's world-famous Archaeology and Palaeontology departments, which drew on the work of renowned scientists Raymond Dart and Phillip Tobias, among others, continue to play a leading part in excavations of the site, and Wits retains ownership of Sterkfontein's intellectual rights. In recent years, Professor Lee Berger made two significant discoveries in the Cradle of Humankind World Heritage Site

Panoramic view of Wits' East and West Campuses, linked by the AMIC deck bridging the M1 highway. Photo: Shivan Parusnath

– *Australopithecus sediba* in 2010 and *Homo naledi* in 2015. Six years later, in 2021, Berger and his team announced the discovery of 'Leti', the skull of a *Homo naledi* child found in a remote passage of the Rising Star cave system. Almost 2 000 individual fragments of more than two dozen individuals at all life stages of *Homo naledi* have been recovered since the Rising Star cave system was discovered in 2013, making this the richest site for fossil hominins in Africa.

'OPEN UNIVERSITIES SOUTH AFRICA'

After gaining power in 1948, the National Party government began to extend measures to segregate educational institutions and curricula – including the segregation of universities. In response, in 1957, Wits, the University of Cape Town, Rhodes University and the University of Natal issued a joint statement titled 'The Open Universities in South Africa', committing the institutions to the principles of university autonomy and academic freedom.

Throughout the years of the apartheid regime (1948–1993), the Wits community protested strongly and continued to maintain a firm, consistent and vigorous stand against apartheid. As time went by, more civil liberties were withdrawn in the country and peaceful opposition to apartheid was suppressed. The consequences for the University's continual protests and opposition to apartheid constraints were severe. Banning, the deportation and detention of students and staff, as well as frequent invasions of the campus by riot police to disrupt peaceful protest meetings were commonplace.

In 1959, the apartheid government's Extension of University Education Act forcibly restricted the registration of Black students for most of the apartheid era. Wits protested strongly and continued to maintain its firm, consistent opposition to apartheid. This marked the beginning of a period of conflict with the apartheid regime, which coincided with a period of massive growth for the University.

The University was not wholly united in its opposition to apartheid at this point. This stemmed from the Wits Council being dominated by conservative mining and financial interests, compounded by the fact that the former provided major financial support to the University (as it had done from the very beginning). This internal tension would characterise the University until the 1990s.

The 1980s was a period of heightened opposition to apartheid, as Wits struggled to maintain its autonomy in the face of attacks from the apartheid state. As the apartheid government attempted, through the threat of financial sanctions, to bring Wits under firmer control, protests escalated, culminating in the General Assembly of 28 October 1987, at which Wits reiterated its commitment to the values underlying the 'Open Universities' statement, and to which the University of the Western Cape now added its voice.

University management also came under increasing pressure to implement change within Wits. Many disadvantaged communities and political organisations such as the then banned African National Congress (ANC) perceived Wits as an elitist institution dominated by white interests. It was necessary to further transform Wits, and this evolution continues today through curriculum reform,

Prior to the Extension of University Education Act 45 of 1959, Wits and the University of Cape Town operated as open universities. Their criteria for admission were purely academic and did not consider race, colour or creed. Source: University of the Witwatersrand's Central Records Office and Archives

diversifying the academy and the student body, and renaming Wits' places and spaces, amongst other transformation initiatives.

AN INTELLECTUAL HOTBED

Wits has been fortunate to attract some of the most influential academics, intellectuals, scientists and researchers in the country. As a centre of academic and research excellence, the University has a long and distinguished record. From developing and constructing vital radar equipment in the Second World War to being the first African university to own a computer, from producing a systematic climatological atlas of southern Africa to achieving a successful graft of plastic cornea, there can be no dispute that Wits has always been at the forefront of technological advancement. The country's first dental hospital and school were established at Wits, as were the departments of Physiotherapy and Occupational Therapy. Wits was the first South African institution to open a clinic for the treatment of speech defects, the first blood transfusion service in the country was started by its medical students, and the University's scholars have greatly advanced the theory of human origins and evolution.

The stories of many of these achievements – from original patents to medical breakthroughs, from significant historical and anthropological discoveries to Nobel Prize awards – are reflected in the pages of this book, and hundreds more can be found on the Wits website.

WITS AS AN OPEN UNIVERSITY

Benedict Vilakazi is often celebrated as the first Black academic to be employed in a teaching capacity at a university in South Africa. He arrived at Wits in 1935 with a BA from Unisa, completed his honours and master's degrees by 1938, and earned his doctorate in 1946. Despite already being an acclaimed Zulu novelist and poet, he was only offered the lowly position of a language assistant to Professor CM Doke, the then head of the Department of Bantu Studies. It was Doke who had strongly urged his appointment because he felt that 'for the proper teaching of Bantu languages at the University, an African Native Assistant is needed'.[5] His appointment stirred considerable public criticism and opposition from the University's hierarchy, many of whom supported the then widely held ideology of racial segregation. Vilakazi, undeterred, went on to publish widely in a new, syncretic form of poetry he had developed, combining praise poetry and blank verse, as well as academic articles. He died prematurely, aged only 41.

The extraordinary Mary Susan Malahlela-Xakana was the first Black woman to register as a medical doctor in South Africa after qualifying from Wits in 1947. She was also the first recipient of the Native Trust Fund to study medicine, which had been open to Black students at Wits from 1941. Malahlela-Xakana was a founding member of the Young Women's Christian Association (YWCA), a member of the Women's Peace Movement and a member of the Fort Hare University Council. She participated in community work for 34 years of her life.

A far more recent medical first for Wits was when Dr Nolubabalo Unati Nqebelele became, in 2018, the first Black woman in South Africa to earn a PhD in internal medicine, becoming a specialist in chronic kidney disease. She is one of a very select group of such specialists in the country. One of South Africa's youngest inspirational medical graduates, Dr Thakgalo Thibela, who hails from the rural village of Violetbank in Mpumalanga, turned 21 in 2021, and serves at the Helen Joseph Hospital, one of Wits' teaching platforms.

Today, Wits is proud to have a string of Black leaders at its helm. At present, Dr Judy Dlamini serves as the chancellor of the University. She is a medical doctor by training and is also a leading businesswoman, entrepreneur, author and philanthropist. She succeeded the Honourable Justice Dikgang Moseneke and the Honourable Justice Richard Goldstone, both former Constitutional Court luminaries.

Professor Zeblon Zenzele Vilakazi is the current vice-chancellor and principal of the University. He succeeded Professor Adam Habib (2013–2020) and Professor Loyiso Nongxa (2002–2012), who served in this role for seven and ten years respectively.

ACTIVISM
In the decades of the 1970s and 1980s, political activism and mobilisation against apartheid defined a large part of the Wits identity. Many anti-apartheid activists of the period were associated with the University. Trade unionist and medical doctor Neil Aggett worked closely with the Wits student leadership of the 1970s. He was detained for 70 days, assaulted and tortured

Dr Judy Dlamini was elected as the chancellor of Wits University on 31 July 2018. Source: University of the Witwatersrand's Central Records Office and Archives

by the apartheid state's Security Branch police, and then found dead – hanged in his prison cell – on 5 February 1982. He was 28 years old. His death was never properly resolved, and a reopened inquest into the case in 2020 brought many Wits alumni and staff to the stand. Included were Barbara Hogan, Auret van Heerden, Clive van Heerden, Keith Coleman, Ismail Momoniat, Maurice Smithers and Firoz Cachalia, an alumnus and now a law professor and director of the Mandela Institute at Wits.

Another long-time anti-apartheid activist, who was influential in the United Democratic Front (UDF) during the 1980s, was David Webster, a lecturer in the Anthropology Department. Webster was assassinated at his home in Troyeville on 1 May 1989. Many other Witsies were questioned, incarcerated and sometimes paid the ultimate price. Ruth First was such an activist – she was killed by a parcel bomb in Mozambique in 1982. Today, the University hosts the annual Ruth First Lecture in her honour.

And yet, while Wits students and staff organised and resisted apartheid as part of the opposition in wider South African society, a struggle of a different kind was under way in the University. For many Black students at Wits in the 1980s – still in a minority because they required ministerial permission to be able to attend the institution – being at Wits was an opportunity to organise around Black political issues, as in the case of the racially exclusive Black Students'

OVERVIEW

Left to right: Deputy Vice-Chancellor Professor Yunus Ballim, Professor Phillip Tobias, and Vice-Chancellor and Principal Professor Loyiso Nongxa participate in an academic anti-xenophobia march at Wits, close to Jan Smuts Avenue, held on 21 May 2008. Source: Wits Communications

One of the many anti-apartheid student protests during the 1970s and 1980s. Source: Wits Communications

ORIGINS

Students and staff gather at the East Campus lawns to pay respects to the 'gentle hero' following David Webster's assassination on 1 May 1989. A student residence on the West Campus cluster was named the David Webster Hall of Residence in 1992. Source: University of the Witwatersrand's Central Records Office and Archives

Society (BSS). Non-racialism under the banner of organisations like the UDF was the dominant oppositional discourse. The exclusively Black and radicalised BSS flew in the face of this ideal on campus, putting forward the viewpoint that non-racialism was only possible in a free society, and that the University was still part of apartheid South Africa. Black students on campus at the time, commuting from the surrounding townships, brought a militant style of protest compared to that to which most white students were accustomed. Protests on campus were common during the 1980s, as were police invasions – there were 52 police raids of the University between 1986 and 1988 alone.

On-campus tensions ran high as the white, government-funded, conservative Students' Moderate Alliance (SMA) began to deliberately provoke increasingly violent clashes with the BSS. All the while, the University's officials had to examine their commitments to independence and protest without facilitating potentially deadly clashes.

The year 1990 was a turning point for Wits, when a decision on a new way forward had to be made to help build a new South Africa. An era in the University's history came to an end when, in that year, the National Union of South African Students (NUSAS), the major non-racial anti-apartheid student organisation, and BSS leaders were called to a late-night meeting at Wits, where they were addressed by former president Nelson Mandela. He instructed them to disband their existing structures and to form a non-racial, national student body. The BSS at Wits called a referendum in which 75 per cent of its members voted in support of the consolidated student body. This paved the way for the development of the contemporary identity that Wits has taken in the twenty-first century – more representative of the country's demographics and more responsive to historical imbalances and injustices.

HOW FAR WE'VE COME

Wits has its historical origins in the mining industry, and it is undeniably a defining part of the City it calls home, but in many significant ways it has never been constrained by either mining or Johannesburg. Its beginnings are steeped in the liberal tradition, academic excellence, civic activism, and a commitment to the political, social and intellectual independence of the institution. The stories that follow reflect this diversity and the pursuit of excellence.

WE LEAD CHANGE

The Last Word: Benedict Vilakazi

Benedict Wallet Vilakazi (1906–1947), affectionately celebrated as the father of Nguni literature and the founder of modern Zulu poetry, was the first Black person in South Africa to receive a doctorate in literature. He was also the first Black person in the then Union of South Africa to teach at a white university. He has a street named after him in Soweto. Yet, outside his body of literary and academic work, little is known about the man behind the words.

Portrait of Dr Benedict Wallet Vilakazi.
Source: Museum Africa

IN SEARCH OF VILAKAZI

Khulani Vilakazi, the poet's grandson, said in a 2006 interview with the *Mail & Guardian* that his family was still trying to understand more about his grandfather. 'The family does not know him that much, he died when my father was about four years old [and] my father died when I was three. So, it is difficult for us as a family to produce personal anecdotes about what type of man he was. [He] never had enough time with his family.'[6] What is clear is that Vilakazi was on a personal quest to preserve and develop the Zulu language. 'He saw himself as being sent by the ancestors [for this purpose]. His poem 'Ngizwa Ingoma' speaks to that notion, of a person anointed,' said Khulani.

Indeed, Vilakazi cut himself off from his birthplace, family and ancestors when he moved to Johannesburg at the age of 29 to pursue his academic career and he would lament this in much of his poetry. Part of his poem 'Wo, Ngitshele Mntanomlungu' describes the move:

Ungiletheleni lapha?
(Why have you brought me here?)
Ngingen' amadol' angisinde
(I enter with heavy knees)
Ngicabang' ikhanda lizule
(I think and my head spins).

Vilakazi's childhood was spent herding cattle and, until the age of ten, attending the local mission school. He then transferred to a co-educational Roman Catholic secondary school. After completing his schooling, he trained as a teacher and then taught at the Ohlange Institute in Phoenix near Durban. Studying on his own, he earned a BA degree in African studies with distinction from Unisa in 1934, with special work on the Zulu language.

He was initiated as an *imbongi*, a traditional composer, in the Zondi clan. His birthplace of KwaDukuza, close to the main headquarters of the nineteenth-century Zulu king Shaka kaSenzangakhona, provided Vilakazi with imagery for his poetry. He was determined to cement the Zulu language as a mighty force – as King Shaka did with his people.

Scan of title page of one of the poetry collections of Dr Benedict Wallet Vilakazi – Amal'eZulu – a classic in African literature. Source: Wits University Press

Vilakazi Street in Soweto, named after the poet, is also famous as the street on which both former president and alumnus Nelson Mandela and Archbishop Desmond Tutu lived. Photo: Daniel Born

GROUNDBREAKING WORK

Wits University Press (WUP), which is the oldest university press in South Africa (established in 1922), published Vilakazi's first book of poems, *Inkondlo kaZulu*, in 1935. By then, he was already well known as a poet and a writer and his works had been published in various journals and newspapers such as *The Star*, *UmAfrika* and *The Bantu World*. Coincidentally, Wits was looking for an assistant in the Department of African Languages at the time, and Vilakazi was appointed as language assistant to Professor CM Doke, head of the department, that same year.

WUP published Vilakazi's second volume of poetry, *Amal'eZulu* (1945), as well as the first Zulu-English dictionary, which Vilakazi compiled in collaboration with Doke. In 1946, he received a doctorate in literature from Wits.

Vilakazi also published three novels in the 1930s: *Noma Nini!* (Mariannhill Mission Press), *Udingiswayo KaJobe* (Sheldon Press) and *Nje Nempela* (Mariannhill Mission Press). His volumes of poetry and novels are all on the list of required reading in Zulu literature courses.

'The time has now come to end any discrimination in my department on the grounds of race or colour.' Professor Clement M Doke

Through his writing, Vilakazi became a spokesperson for his people, though he was never overtly political. He often articulated social issues that remain relevant today, including the safety of Black miners, the plight of the poor, and the impact of industrial advancement on human values. These are still societal challenges that

the University is tackling today – for example, through the Wits DigiMine, the Southern Centre for Inequality Studies, and the use of new digital technologies to advance humanity.

CONTINUOUS STRUGGLE

Despite his success, Vilakazi faced discrimination and criticism. His appointment at Wits was opposed by conservative whites who could not come to terms with an African man lecturing white students. He was also scorned and ridiculed by Black people, who wrote letters of discontent to newspapers condemning Vilakazi for consenting to be used by whites through such a 'collaborationist appointment', as Dumisane Krushchev Ntshangase wrote in a 1995 paper for the Wits Institute for Advanced Social Research.

Professor Humphrey R Raikes, the then principal of Wits, personally wrote a letter to Vilakazi to explain his position at his new job. He would be a junior academic staff member, would look after the 'Native library' and would take care of African students only. He would not be allowed to teach, grade or supervise white students unless they asked for help in their Zulu courses.

In a letter in the Wits Archives, dated January 1947, Doke wrote to the Human Resources Department that 'the time has now come to end any discrimination in my department on the grounds of race or colour', requesting that Vilakazi's status be changed to that of lecturer.

In October that same year, Vilakazi died suddenly of meningitis. He was survived by five children, who attended his funeral at Mariannhill along with thousands of people.

In their collaborative dictionary, published a year after Vilakazi's death, Doke wrote: '[The] sudden death of Dr Vilakazi, cut off amid further research and literary activity, has deprived the African people of a brilliant son, one who not only achieved high academic standing but whose life and personality gained for him a lasting place in their affections. This dictionary of his mother-tongue – the language he loved – will stand as a monument to a great African.'[7]

Vilakazi was born Bhambatha ka Mshini and changed his name to Benedict Wallet after converting to Roman Catholicism. At his mother's insistence, he kept the family name Vilakazi.

Vilakazi spent some time at Mariannhill training for the priesthood, but his fascination was an intellectual rather than a spiritual one – he soon changed his vocation to that of a writer.

The Order of Ikhamanga (Gold) was conferred on Vilakazi posthumously in 2016 for 'his exceptional contribution to the field of literature in indigenous languages and the preservation of isiZulu culture'.

WITS PIONEER: JOHNNY CLEGG

Becoming the White Zulu

It was October 1976, with the Soweto uprising fresh in the country's memory, and David Coplan, now emeritus professor in social anthropology at Wits, found himself in solitary confinement at The Old Fort prison after being arrested during a music performance in Tembisa, a township just outside Johannesburg.

Authorities would visit his good friend Johnny Clegg, who himself saw the inside of several jail cells for defying cultural boundaries at the time. Clegg's insistence that Coplan was 'an American idiot' who simply didn't understand the laws would help gain Coplan his freedom several weeks later. 'Johnny was loyal to a fault,' says Coplan of the legendary musician.

Immersed in the study of Zulu history and culture, Johnny Clegg left an unforgettable rhythmic expression of South African cultural fluidity and appreciation. Photo: David Redfern/Getty Images

ORIGINS

'He was always part of the Wits family. There exists such a thing.' Professor David Coplan

The two men had met a year earlier, when Coplan, a graduate student in ethnomusicology at Indiana University in the US, came to South Africa to research a documentary about township music. 'I heard of this white guy who speaks Zulu and has a Zulu band. I went to see him at Wits, where he was studying anthropology, and there was this immediate sense of kinship. We were both musicians looking for a way to cross cultural boundaries. Johnny was trying to beat the drum for the value of all cultures in the country. He was so energetic, so enthusiastic, it just gobbled me up.'

Clegg was one half of the as-yet-unknown acoustic duo Juluka with Sipho Mchunu, and the two would search for any opportunity to perform – in contravention of apartheid laws.

Before the fame that followed Juluka's debut album in 1979, Clegg poured his love of South African cultures into anthropology, becoming a lecturer at Wits and writing several seminal papers. On weekends, he would take part in dance competitions as a certified member of a Zulu dance team.

'We were full of beans, just young men on the loose, wanting to go to vibrant townships even though we weren't allowed. Johnny's performances

were so athletic, persuasive, and African people went crazy for it – seeing someone take their culture seriously, in composition, singing, lecturing, Zulu guitar and dance. We stuck out like sore thumbs, but back then the only people you feared were the police,' says Coplan.

Coplan was deported in 1977 and could not come back to South Africa for 14 years, but he and Clegg stayed in touch. '[Johnny] came to the States often on tour and I would always see his shows. We'd stay up talking until the wee hours. He needed an ear – in those days, he was arrested so often in his own country, but he wasn't going to give up.'

Coplan became head of the Anthropology Department at Wits in 1996 and Clegg would often visit (in between averaging around 180 performances a year). Clegg also donated money in memory of his mentor in the department, Professor David Webster, who was assassinated by apartheid security forces in 1989. '[Johnny] was always part of the Wits family. There exists such a thing,' Coplan adds.

Clegg never wavered in his goal to bring people and cultures together. On his final tour before succumbing to pancreatic cancer in 2019, he had no illusions that this would be the end, says Coplan. 'He'd undergone terrifying treatments, and yet still put on this incredible, energetic tour. But he knew it was the last squeeze of the lemon. "So, I'll kill myself saying goodbye to our people," he said. He is, in a word, my hero.'

South African musician Johnny Clegg (1953–2019), a Wits alumnus, challenged South Africa's apartheid regime through his music and promoted racial reconciliation. Photo: Peter Maher

Juluka performed their hits including 'Impi' and 'Scatterlings of Africa' in the US, Canada, the UK, France, Germany and Scandinavia. After the group had disbanded, Clegg formed the nine-piece band Savuka in 1987, which sold over one million copies of their debut album and produced hits like 'Asimbonanga' and 'Great Heart'.

Johnny Clegg received numerous awards for his contribution to music and society, notably the Knight of Arts and Letters from the French government in 1991, the Order of Ikhamanga (Silver) from the South African government in 2012 and the Order of the British Empire in 2015.

Johnny had two sons – Jaron and Jesse Clegg. The latter is also a popular musician and Wits graduate. Wits gets multiple mentions in *Scattering of Africa: My Early Years*, a book published in 2021 that tells the story of Johnny Clegg in his own voice.

Another famous Wits graduate is songwriter and musician Claire Johnston, the lead singer of Mango Groove. Born out of a band formed by three Wits students, Mango Groove fuses pop and township music.

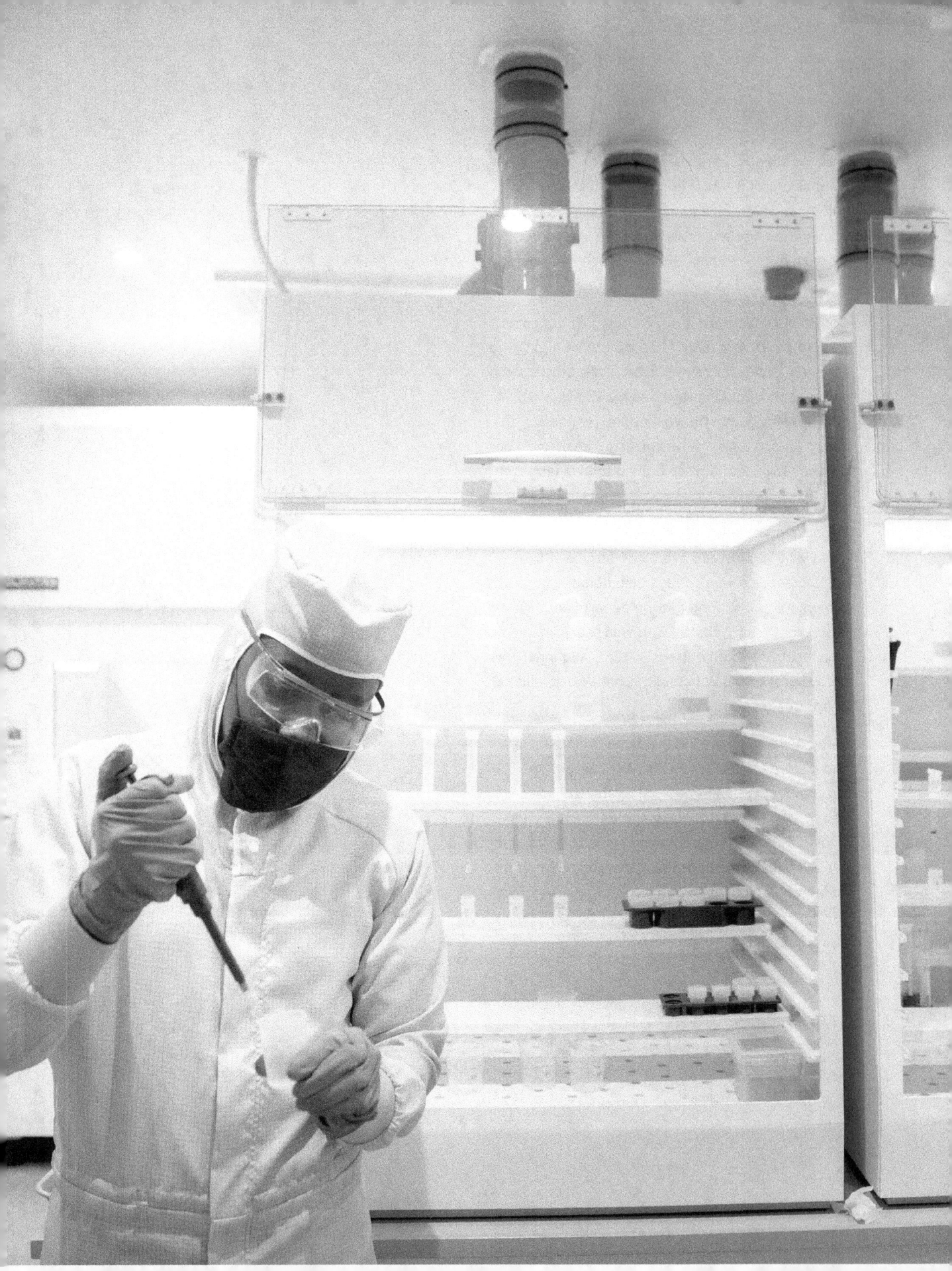

WE HARNESS THE POWER OF PLACE

Dynamite Underground: Wits Geosciences

The Witwatersrand has produced much of the world's gold – some estimates claim over 40 000 tonnes were mined from the region's rich ore deposits. Were it not for Wits' contribution to geosciences, this would not have been possible, says Professor Gillian Drennan, head of the School of Geosciences and a member of the newly formed Wits Earth Sciences cluster.

Wits, which started as a mining college, was born of necessity as South Africa became a recognised force in the global mining industry. What happened here was very different from the scene in the Northern Hemisphere, where mining was more of a continuation of the discovery of natural history. In South Africa, it was driven by the mineral wealth of the country and it established the foundations of the economy.

Wits' focus was on science for industry. As mines became deeper, gold was found in pyrite (called 'fool's gold' for its superficial resemblance to gold). Understanding geochemical relationships between gold and pyrite was essential in extracting as much gold as possible from pyrite through chemical processes.

The Wits Isotope Geoscience Laboratory (WIGL) is the first of its kind in Africa. Normal air contains over one million particles per cubic foot, but the complex air filtration system in the WIGL reduces this by about a million times. Along with a completely metal-free environment – everything in the lab is constructed of durable, acid-resistant plastic – the air quality ensures that any sensitive samples processed in the WIGL remain contamination-free. Photo: Daniel Born

ORIGINS

'It's in our nature to be adventurous and willing to question things.' Professor Gillian Drennan

ON THE FRONTIER

The School of Geosciences remained at the forefront of research and training, serving the mining sector and related areas. Today it is the largest and most diverse academic earth sciences institution in Africa. The school is also home to the Wits Isotope Geosciences Laboratory and the Seismic Research Centre. It co-hosts the Centre of Excellence in Mineral and Energy Analysis and the Centre of Excellence in Palaeosciences. Wits is the only university in the country that provides postgraduate training in palaeosciences and geophysics.

The School of Geosciences works closely with the School of Mining Engineering. In the past ten years, Wits has established the Wits Mining Institute, the Centre for Mechanised Mining Systems, the Wits DigiMine, and the Centre for Sustainability in Mining and Industry, amongst other entities, in the Faculty of Engineering and the Built Environment.

'We've grown into a multidisciplinary institution while maintaining our roots in economic geology,' says Drennan. 'The reason that the School of Geosciences has done so well, I believe, is because we have a strong heritage and enthusiastic academics and professional and administrative staff. It's in our nature to be adventurous and willing to question things, and to stick our necks out to test hypotheses.'

The school has a surprising history of breaking cultural boundaries and stereotypes. While it used to be a male-dominated field, today more than 50 per cent of undergraduates and half the staff are female. 'I'm proud to be part of that legacy, as the first female head of the school. What an awe-inspiring opportunity to embrace a new way forward and to foster change and adaptation as we move into the Fourth Industrial Revolution,' says Drennan. 'When geoscientists are out in the field, sitting around a campfire, we are all hot and sweaty together,' she adds. 'There's no room for airs and graces.'

LIGHT IN THE DARK

Professor Musa Manzi, director of the Wits Seismic Research Centre, broke barriers when he became the first Black South African to obtain a PhD in geophysics. The first in his family to finish matric, Manzi describes the beginning of his journey: 'I asked my mom for R95 for a bus ticket to Johannesburg from our rural village in KwaZulu-Natal,' he says. 'I had no idea how to apply to study, we did not have the Internet, but I knew that I wanted to go to Wits to study science.'

His seven distinctions in matric afforded him a R7 000 bursary, but for his first year of study he slept in a lab while working towards a general BSc. 'Friends let me shower and eat at their residences.' The hardship paid off, Manzi says. 'I used all my spare time to study.' He fell in love with geophysics and obtained his PhD in 2012, specialising in reflection seismology. His passion for his field is visible as he describes the process. 'Reflection seismology uses seismic waves to search for oil, gas and minerals beneath the Earth's surface. The waves are sent

'We want to demonstrate that geology is not just about mining, but an essential component in many diverse fields – from climate change and environmental studies to food security and water management.'
Professor Gillian Drennan

from the surface to the Earth's crust, around 11 kilometres deep, and we analyse the data to determine changes in rock properties. It's used to indicate which rocks host minerals, and also to improve mine safety.'

Manzi's PhD thesis became the basis of several subsequent studies to identify areas in mines that may be prone to methane gas explosions. It received the award for the best paper published in geophysics from the Society of Exploration Geophysicists, with Manzi becoming the first African winner. He became a lecturer and associate professor and established the Wits Seismic Research Centre in 2015 – the only training hub of its kind in Africa. He is the recipient of two prestigious National Science and Technology Forum Awards, the latter awarded to his team in 2021.

ONWARDS AND DOWNWARDS

Manzi explains why reflection seismology technology must go underground. 'South Africa has the deepest mines in the world and the further our seismic waves travel, the worse the resolution of the data becomes. We're now developing innovative, cost-effective and environmentally friendly ways to conduct seismic surveys inside mining tunnels to improve accuracy.'

The first Black South African to obtain a PhD in geophysics, Professor Musa Manzi made his mark by establishing the Wits Seismic Research Centre in 2015. Photos: Daniel Born

ORIGINS

Professor Gillian Drennan marvels at an extremely rare crystalline gold piece on quartz. Photo: Daniel Born

For her part, Drennan is both forward and downward looking. 'Do not listen to those who say the heyday of gold is over,' she says. 'Gold and other minerals are still vital as we enter the Fourth Industrial Revolution. Technology cannot exist without it – a smartphone contains over 40 elements that come from mined minerals. Increasingly, rare earth elements that occur in very small amounts will need to be mined. The challenge is to repurpose ourselves. New minerals need to be found to support technology, in sufficient quantities, while being as environmentally friendly as possible.'

Drennan believes that artificial intelligence is not the threat that it is touted to be. 'It's about adapting and using technology to our advantage. Current research in the school includes the use of high-speed computing to look for new minerals and to look at historical data in new ways. We use drones as tools to explore inaccessible areas while doing fieldwork. Our second- and third-year students now have access to ruggedised tablets that can be dropped without breaking, which have the ability to superimpose various levels of data gathered in the field, and which form a detailed 3D picture in real time.'

Drennan is of the firm view that teaching, too, will have to adapt to the needs of newer generations. 'Previous generations of geoscientists believed in exploring outdoors and specialising in one field, but things are changing. Nowadays, students prefer to work on computers and want to follow several careers in their lifetime. In addition to developing an understanding of the necessity for fieldwork, the challenge is developing a broad skills set for students that applies to different industries and career paths.' With a subtle mind shift, she believes, the future is a world of opportunity rather than a threat – just as Wits' predecessors believed when the University was founded 100 years ago.

South Africa has the deepest and most stressed mines in the world – some as deep as four kilometres below sea level. Addressing the unique and complex challenges they bring has put Wits at the forefront of mining research in the world.

In 2022, Wits students may participate in a global Hyperloop competition led by Elon Musk's Boring Company, a division of which is headed by Daniel Frolich, a Wits engineer who also works at SpaceX. The challenge is for students to dig as deep as possible, quickly – skills taught in Wits' Geosciences and Mining Engineering schools. According to Musk's father, Elon was first introduced to computers at a Wits workshop at the age of 12.

WE CREATE AND APPLY KNOWLEDGE

Fighting the Good Fight

Founded in 1978 by Professor John Dugard as a legal research unit within Wits University, the Centre for Applied Legal Studies (CALS) encouraged law reform and improved access to justice during the apartheid era. Despite undergoing changes over the years, this public interest legal organisation in the Wits School of Law remains committed to promoting human rights and challenging systems of power in South Africa.

Students, candidate attorneys, researchers, academics and lawyers often meet at Wits to discuss legal issues. This picture is taken outside the entrance to the School of Law. Photo: Shivan Parusnath

The Wits Law Clinic is the litigation arm of CALS, registered with the Legal Practice Council, which represents underserved and indigent communities in the country, thereby using academia to advance social justice.

The high cost of legal representation often creates a barrier for oppressed people seeking to access legal assistance when they have been victims of injustice or when their rights have been violated. Attorney Thandeka Kathi explains the core purpose of the centre and its demands: 'To deliver an inclusive and equal society, we need to have a heart for the downtrodden, inexhaustible grit and committed funds.'

It is hearing their clients' stories, whether they have suffered social, economic or political injustice, that motivates the centre's staff

'To deliver an inclusive and equal society, we need to have a heart for the downtrodden, inexhaustible grit, and committed funds.' Thandeka Kathi

members to act. Their programmes include those related to business and human rights; civil and political justice; environmental justice; gender justice; and home, land and rural democracy, which promotes their clients' access to basic socio-economic rights, including the right to sufficient water, adequate housing, and protection from subjective eviction.

In its earlier days, the CALS was instrumental in deconstructing the legacy of apartheid when it worked under the radar to support anti-apartheid activists. During the #FeesMustFall protests, the organisation represented nearly 50 students from the University of Johannesburg, providing legal support and making bail applications on their behalf.

CALS HAS AGENCY

During the 2020/21 coronavirus lockdown, when large gatherings were illegal, protests took a different form. Nationally, people from the entertainment and hospitality industries came together to participate in peaceful protests, such as the 'Million Seats on the Streets' demonstration and the #JobsSavesLives movement, acting in solidarity against crippling lockdown regulations. While the #BlackLivesMatter movement received much attention in the US, South Africans also acted within their constitutional rights to express their dissatisfaction.

Palesa Madi, the deputy director at CALS, says, 'We have challenged and held to account systems that perpetuate harm, poverty, inequality and human rights violations. We

The Centre for Applied Legal Studies exists to represent the underserved and indigent communities in the country. Photo: Siphiwe Sibeko/REUTERS

Preparing for a challenge in the centre's boardroom. Photo: Shivan Parusnath

'We are effective when we are creative. Our non-traditional lawyering explores other disciplines to inform our work and makes us better human rights lawyers.' Palesa Madi

'We will continue to use research, litigation and advocacy to strengthen our relationships with social movements and activists, and to hold the state and corporations accountable for human rights violations.' Palesa Madi

often work with radical movements and activists, whom we represent when they exercise their constitutional right to protest.' Madi suggests that a nuanced understanding of protests to challenge the perception that they are illegal and violent is urgently needed, because the media often portrays protesters in this light, without covering the actual essence of the story.

FINDING NEW WAYS
As a result of the global Covid-19 pandemic, digital activism has surged, with more than four million people signing up to protest for equality around gender-related issues. The CALS has moved in this direction by using social media to call for various actions from those abusing human rights. Using an online platform, the centre frequently asks people to endorse statements, sign petitions and make use of hashtags to mobilise certain movements. As Madi explains, 'We are effective when we are creative. Our non-traditional lawyering explores other disciplines to inform our work and to make us better human rights lawyers.'

The CALS is funded by several foundations and donors, allowing it to deliver on its mandate to reconstruct an inclusive and equal society. Strategic litigation has allowed the centre to create broader social impact and to take on cases that have changed national laws.

Aligned with Wits University's history in the mining sector, CALS made submissions to the mining sector and the state to support the needs of mine workers, especially around their obligation to test and screen miners for

Covid-19 and to provide quarantine facilities and transportation. This appeal was brought to the mining sector by the centre on behalf of community networks.

In another example of fighting the good fight concerning the unprecedented pandemic and the loss of income experienced by many due to the 2020 hard lockdown, the CALS made submissions to the state, forcing a moratorium on evictions. The national impact of this resulted in many poor people being able to escape displacement, which, in turn, preserved their dignity.

These critical changes to the lockdown regulations forged a stronger relationship between the centre and the state, says Madi, and set the tone for increased engagement and collaboration. The partnership will benefit the state through capacity building and a stronger reliance on the academy to provide research, which will move the state's legal system further into the future. 'We will continue to use research, litigation and advocacy to strengthen our relationships with social movements and activists, and to hold the state and corporations accountable for human rights violations.'

Such collaborations to benefit indigent communities have both national and global impacts. In 2013, in response to a request from the UN Working Group on Business and Human Rights for proposals to develop implementation guidelines for National Action Plans (NAPs) on business and human rights, the CALS led a coalition of African and Asian researchers at the Singapore Management University. This global collaborative project shared perspectives on NAPs from key players in the Global South, to support the working group's mission to embed NAPs in the regions. The research work put the Global South on the map with regard to equality for NAPs in terms of business and human rights.

PRACTISING WHAT YOU PREACH

Whilst the CALS prioritises the development of all marginalised and disadvantaged people, a deliberate approach is taken to break down those barriers that continue to disadvantage Black women in particular. Policies developed by the centre are embedded in the University's recruitment processes to attract, retain and advance Black female employees.

The centre keeps hope alive for the vulnerable through its steadfast fight for equality and justice. CALS' courage is evident in the way it holds business, the state and those in power to account.

The CALS has been innovative in using video and different media to distribute information to those affected by human rights violations and in so doing is able to bridge the gaps between people who speak different languages.

Dr Stephen Matseoane attended the Shared Interest 2018 Annual Spring Benefit at the Edison Ballroom on 20 March 2018 in New York City. Photo: Ben Gabbe/Getty Images

WITS PIONEER: STEPHEN MATSEOANE

From Bara to the Bronx

Stephen Matseoane decided to become a doctor when he was still a youngster playing soccer in the streets of Alexandra township outside Johannesburg. 'Every time I injured myself, which was quite frequently, I'd head to the local clinic to get stitched up. Wits students and staff ran it and their work made such an impression on me,' he remembers.

Little did he know how much determination it would take to overcome the difficulties imposed on a Black South African medical student in the 1950s and 1960s. Mr Matseoane Senior was an informal trader who would wake daily at 3 am to sell *vetkoek* (traditional South African fried dough bread) and Stephen's mother was a domestic worker. The family house had no running water and paying for higher education was out of the question. 'It took a lot of hard work, but I was accepted to Wits Medical School and the Johannesburg City Council paid for my tuition,' says Matseoane. 'There were three African and five Indian medical students in our year. I felt so lucky to be there and I still do – I had smarter friends who didn't get the opportunity.'

'I only told my parents the day before leaving for the US. My mother sobbed but gave me [her] blessing – they knew how determined I was.' Professor Stephen Matseoane

Reunion of Dr Salome Maswime, Dr Ian Gross and Dr Stephen Matseoane on 9 May 2019, in New York City, at the Wits New York Alumni Reunion. Photo: Jeffrey Vock

Yet, specialising in his chosen field of obstetrics and gynaecology remained out of reach in the country. While completing his internship at Baragwanath Hospital, the administrator told Matseoane that it was simply not possible. 'I was disappointed, but not discouraged. Shortly after, I saw an advertisement from the Bronx Lebanon Hospital in New York looking for medical graduates. I applied and was accepted but couldn't afford the flight. So I found a cargo ship that was transporting oil to the US, asked the captain to take me on board, and he agreed. I only told my parents the day before leaving, as I knew they would want me to stay in Alexandra and practise there. My mother sobbed when I told her, but they both gave me their blessing – they knew how determined I was.'

As the ship left port, reality dawned. 'Only then did I realise that I was leaving my birth country and that I knew nothing of what awaited me. It was a combination of excitement and fear.'

He had no difficulty with the entrance exam for foreign students when he arrived. 'I couldn't believe how easy it was! It was multiple-choice, while our Wits exams required long essays. I never knew how good my education was until then. Wits had given me wings to fly to the US.'

After his residency at the Bronx Lebanon and the Mount Sinai hospitals, Matseoane joined the staff of the Harlem Hospital Center for Obstetrics and Gynaecology at Columbia University. 'Harlem is a major African-American residential and cultural neighbourhood and evoked memories of Baragwanath, Alexandra and Soweto. I felt at home.'

In the late 1990s he was appointed as director of obstetrics and gynaecology at Columbia, as well as president of the New York Gynaecological Society. Now an emeritus professor at Columbia, Matseoane's advice to future students is simple: 'Learn to recognise opportunities, but also work hard. If you don't put in the work, even the most promising career will be short-lived.'

During his tenure at Harlem Hospital, Matseoane introduced several new techniques and procedures to help serve indigent and uninsured patients in the area. He established a family planning clinic in Central Harlem and introduced laparoscopies and colposcopies that would reduce death rates from cervical cancer.

WE ARE GLOBAL

Life as We Know It: The Story of Life

Within a special exhibition case made of reflection-reducing metal oxide glass, locked in a secure, world-class vault at the Wits Evolutionary Studies Institute (ESI), lies the skull of the Taung Child.

The skull of the Taung Child rests in the Phillip V Tobias Fossil Primate and Hominid Laboratory at Wits. Photo: Daniel Born

Identified in 1924 by Professor Raymond Dart, the head of the Anatomy Department at Wits at the time, this skull of a three-year-old child dates back 2.8 million years, and provides the first evidence of early upright walking in a hominid (an early human ancestor). It was the first discovery of an early evolutionary link between apes and humans.

Wits was only two years old then and had barely grown its roots as a mining college, but such a seminal discovery warranted more research and investigation. 'To its credit,' says Professor Bruce Rubidge, director of the Department of Science and Innovation–National Research Foundation Centre of Excellence in Palaeosciences, 'Wits has always been supportive of the palaeosciences and that's why the discipline has flourished at the University, producing some of the world's

Dr Ron Clarke excavating Little Foot at Sterkfontein. Photo: John Hodgkiss

most important finds and research, having accumulated a large collection of fossils before other institutions did.'

Today, the Phillip V Tobias Fossil Primate and Hominid Laboratory houses thousands of fossils on human evolution alongside the Taung skull. The lab is internationally renowned for its collection of Karoo fossil vertebrates, which comprises more than 9 000 catalogued specimens of dinosaurs, therapsids and early mammals. It includes the largest palaeobotany herbarium in the Southern Hemisphere, holding more than 730 000 catalogued specimens of fossil plants and insects. Of special importance are the large collections of fossils from the Cradle of Humankind and other hominid sites.

RARE FINDS

Palaeoanthropological findings, especially of new species, are as scarce as hominid teeth. Professor Lee Berger, Phillip Tobias chair in palaeoanthropology and director of the Centre for the Exploration of the Deep Human Journey at Wits, who is arguably the most prolific palaeoanthropologist still in the field today, found a few hominid teeth in Gladysvale Cave in the Cradle of Humankind in 1991 and then almost nothing for 17 years. 'Some palaeoanthropologists go their entire careers without any significant finds,' he says.

Yet Wits researchers – in both palaeoanthropology and the palaeosciences – are responsible for many of the significant finds in the world.

The seminal finding of the skeleton of Little Foot in 1994, by Ronald Clarke, honorary professor in the Wits Evolutionary Studies Institute, took 15 years to fully excavate, after his initial find of some foot bones at Sterkfontein. At 3.67 million years old, Little Foot (an early *Australopithecus* hominid) is not only one of the most ancient human ancestors discovered, but also one of the most complete – providing a template against which fragment discoveries can be compared and understood. Clarke further learned that Little Foot walked upright and was also capable of climbing trees.

BOUNTIFUL LANDS

'South Africa has delivered a record of life, preserved as fossils, that is more extensive than any other country in the world,' says Rubidge. 'The country has some of the oldest evidence of life, in the form of bacteria and algae, and many subsequent highlights in the development of life

Professor Phillip V Tobias succeeded Professor Raymond Dart as the head of anatomy at Wits and initiated excavation, research and teaching programmes at Sterkfontein. He was one of the country's most decorated scientists and received 3 Nobel Prize nominations, 12 honorary doctorates, and honorary degrees from 17 universities in South Africa, the US, Canada and Europe.

Dr Robert Broom identified and described many mammalian and hominid fossils. His most famous find was 'Mrs Ples', the most complete skull of an *Australopithecus africanus* found in South Africa, at Sterkfontein in 1947. He was awarded an honorary doctorate of science in 1933 by Wits.

Palaeoanthropology involves much more than the hunt for fossils. Wits archaeologist Professor Lyn Wadley from the Wits Evolutionary Studies Institute excavates regularly at Border Cave in the Lebombo Mountains in KwaZulu-Natal. In 2020 she announced that early modern humans cooked starchy food in South Africa 170 000 years ago.

Professor Christopher Henshilwood, South African research chair in The Origins of Modern Human Behaviour at the Evolutionary Studies Institute, continues to make revolutionary discoveries about the origins of modern human culture and technology. These discoveries have helped to restore pride in African people by demonstrating the principal role that Africa played in the evolution of *Homo sapiens*. He also discovered the world's oldest 'hashtag' and the world's oldest jewellery in Blombos Cave in the southern Cape.

Teams from the University of the Witwatersrand excavate the 105 site near Sterkfontein, just outside Johannesburg, on 25 November 2020. Professor Lee Berger and his team have been responsible for some of the most important discoveries about human ancestors in the world.

Photo: Daniel Born

Professor Lee Berger with the cranium of a nearly two-million-year-old Australopithecus sediba. *Photo: Brett Eloff*

'I felt like I'd won the palaeoanthropological lottery.'
Professor Lee Berger

– some of the earliest fish, dinosaurs, therapsids showing the beginning of mammals, and the origins of humans and human technology and culture.'

The Bernard Price Institute for Palaeontological Research (BPI), established at Wits in 1945 through a generous donation from philanthropist Bernard Price, was run by Professor James Kitching. He is still regarded as one of the world's greatest fossil finders. He lived in a tent in the Karoo for more than 23 years while searching the area for fossils. One of his most important finds was when he uncovered the first Karoo vertebrate fossils in Antarctica – which provided critical evidence to show that Antarctica and Africa were once joined in a supercontinent.

The BPI merged with the Wits Institute for Human Evolution in 2013 to form the Evolutionary Studies Institute (ESI), one of the largest palaeosciences research and training centres globally. The current director is Professor Marion Bamford, who is internationally recognised for her pioneering research on fossil wood. The University won the bid to host the nationwide Centre of Excellence in Palaeosciences in 2014 because of its reputation in palaeosciences research.

NEW HORIZONS

The next big hominid discovery following Little Foot came only in 2008, when Professor Lee Berger's then nine-year-old son, Matthew, went to him at a potential new fossil site and said, 'Dad, I found a fossil'. 'I thought, oh, it's probably an antelope,' Berger said, 'but as I walked closer, I knew our lives were going to change. It was a hominid clavicle, and we later found several more hominid fossils there – I felt like I'd won the palaeoanthropological lottery.'

In 2010, the clavicle was identified as belonging to a new species, dating to around 1.98 million years ago. It was named *Australopithecus sediba* and the site, about 15 kilometres from Sterkfontein, was named Malapa.

In 2013, while excavations were on hold to build a lab at Malapa, Berger sent amateur cavers he knew into the Rising Star cave system in the Cradle of Humankind, hoping to find fossils. 'Most of the caves had been well mapped, but they found a chute, just 44 centimetres wide and 12 metres long, and a chamber with bones on the other side. I said, "Oh, great, send me some pictures," then promptly forgot about it.'

When he saw the images, Berger was shocked. 'I was scared, and worried that I was going to stake my reputation on some amateur pictures.'

He made a now-famous Facebook post asking for 'skinny explorers' (because he himself could not fit into the chute) and 60 people applied. 'I chose six people to go exploring and we went live with the discovery where over a million people followed on our social media channels as we discovered over 2 000 specimens.'

In 2015 it was announced that what they had found was a new species, named *Homo naledi*, that lived between 335 000 to 236 000 years ago. Berger was named one of *Time* magazine's 100 most influential people in the world in 2016 because of his find and his contribution to palaeoanthropology.

And he is at it again. In late 2021, Berger and his global team introduced 'Leti' – short for the Setswana word *letimela*, meaning 'the lost one' – a *Homo naledi* child that died when it was approximately four to six years old. No doubt there is more to come from this rich hominid fossil site.

WITS PIONEER: ADVOCATE THULI MADONSELA

A Stalwart of Justice

It was when others turned their backs on her that Advocate Thuli Madonsela found a haven at Wits, her alma mater. 'In the early years of my career I was a trade unionist, but I got demoted because of sexism after I had my first child. So I turned to Wits and they accepted me. There was this ethos of encouraging everyone to create a culture of belonging.'

Advocate Thuli Madonsela addresses the media as the country's Public Protector in 2013. As Public Protector from 2009 to 2016, she served the South African nation with a mandate to strengthen the constitutional democracy of the Republic. Photo: Daniel Born

She joined the Centre for Applied Legal Studies at Wits and, later, the Gender Research Project, while completing her LLB. 'Wits was known as a liberal university and it was important to me to study at an institution that affirms your humanity even though full social inclusion remained elusive – partly because of the broader discriminatory ecosystem and partly because of unexamined unconscious bias,' Madonsela says. 'But they also knew that if you're going to be critical, you must be excellent, and many people at Wits were committed to changing the country and the world. It's maintained that culture of excellence and social justice, and that forms part of the foundation from which I spring.'

'It was important to me to study at an institution that affirms your humanity.'
Thuli Madonsela

As Public Protector from 2009 to 2016, Advocate Madonsela became known as a champion for those who don't have a voice. 'I think [this principle] stems from the combination of gender and race discrimination I've experienced, from knowing how it feels to be "less than".'

As a child, Advocate Madonsela and her extended family of 11 people lived in a four-roomed house in Soweto. She and some siblings slept on straw mattresses in the kitchen when they were home from school for the holidays. Twice, they became victims of forced removals. 'The police would kick residents' doors open in the early hours of the morning,' she recalls. 'I still remember the noise those metal doors made. The grown-ups would hide – it was a traumatic experience.'

She also saw the unfair way in which women were treated under customary law if their husbands died. 'Their house would be taken back, they had fewer rights than minors. If they had a boy, the house was transferred to the son, who could kick his mother out. I saw this happening to neighbours, friends. When the father died, they would disappear.' While working at Wits, her lounge and kitchen were often filled with victims of such evictions. 'Most of my cases were about helping these women who had nowhere to turn.'

Today, Advocate Madonsela is the chair of social justice at Stellenbosch University, where her focus is still on eradicating inequality. 'We're engineering a plan to help South Africa better deal with the transition from an unjust to a just society, using algorithms to track the effects of policy on the ground.'

Madonsela has also discovered mountain climbing as a hobby – which, of course, she uses for good. 'I summited Kilimanjaro on Women's Day in 2019 in aid of Trek for Mandela. In 2020, we climbed Table Mountain to raise funds for students in need as part of the Action4Inclusion campaign. The goal is to summit seven local mountains to raise more funds. It's become a wonderful metaphor for my view on life: if you keep going in the right direction, sticking to your pace, you can heal and change the world around you.'

Advocate Madonsela was awarded an honorary doctorate by Wits in 2017. She also holds honorary doctorates from the universities of Stellenbosch, Cape Town, Fort Hare, Rhodes, North-West and KwaZulu-Natal, and from Canada's Ontario Law Society.

As chief director of transformation and equity in the Department of Justice, Advocate Thuli Madonsela was a technical expert in the drafting of the Constitution, as well as the Promotion of Equality and Prevention of Unfair Discrimination Act, the Employment Equity Act and the Recognition of Customary Marriages Act.

First year science students having a group discussion on the lawns of the Science Stadium on West Campus during a practical session.
Photo: Shivan Parusnath

Photo: Shivan Parusnath

02

Space and Place

OVERVIEW

The philosopher Marc Augé clarifies the difference between a 'space' and a 'place'. Space is only potential – it has yet to be realised by the people and ideas that inhabit it, that bring it to life, that turn it into a 'place'.[8]

In the digital era, the idea of physical space is changing. We need look no further than the Covid-19 pandemic, which forced us to stay and shelter in a place and connect with each other and the economy through online and virtual spaces.

Wits responded to the need for digital transformation in 2016 by providing an inventive physical place, the Tshimologong Digital Innovation Precinct, in Braamfontein. Setswana for 'new beginnings', Tshimologong is an enabling space in which to develop new digital technologies. It was designed for the incubation of digital start-up companies, the commercialisation of research, and the development of high-level digital skills for students, working professionals and unemployed youth. It takes Wits' idea of spaces and places into the future and is one of the University's priority areas discussed in the next chapter.

THE CASE OF THE RAND SHOWGROUNDS

The University's Braamfontein Campus West is a major precinct which houses some schools based in the Faculty of Commerce, Law and Management, and the Faculty of Engineering and the Built Environment. The campus only became part of the University's property in the early 1980s. The site's early history is interesting, colourful and not without some dramatic historical moments.

The original site, Milner Park, belonged to the Witwatersrand Agricultural Society for most of the twentieth century. It was named after Lord Alfred Milner, a former South African High Commissioner, who was instrumental in acquiring the site from the City and allocating it to the society. The society mounted a prestigious annual agricultural show, which attracted celebrities and British royalty, and which eventually became known as the Rand Easter Show. The most significant event at the site was its hosting of the 1936 Empire Exhibition, which showcased the best of the British Commonwealth, including some of South Africa's most important modern art of the time, such as the work of Irma Stern and Alexis Preller.

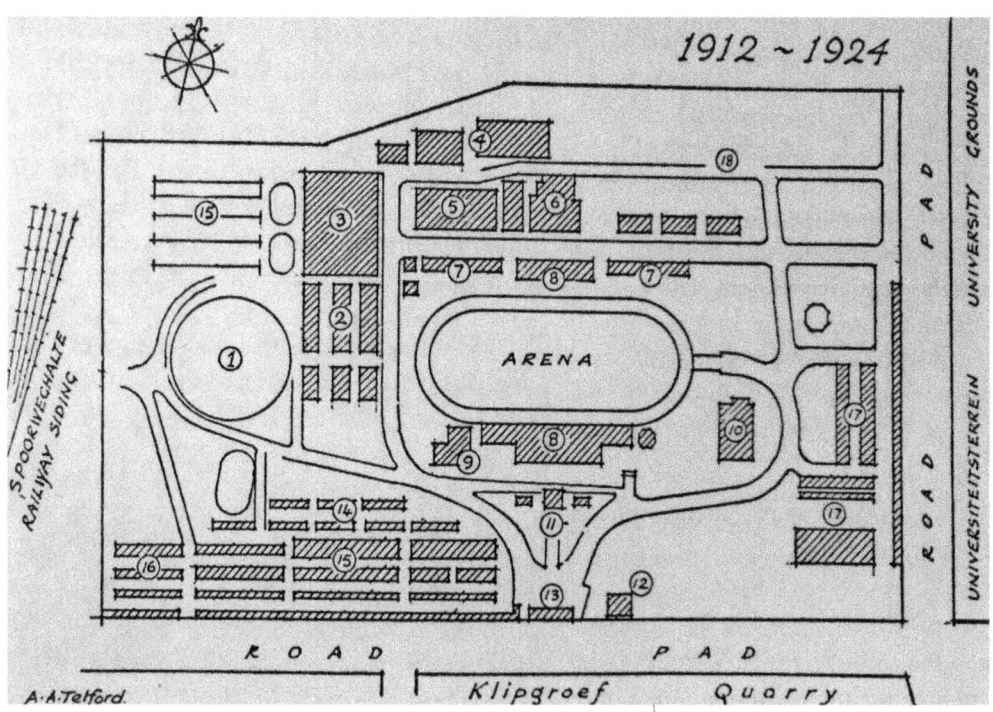

The centrepiece of the exhibition was the Tower of Light, constructed specifically for the exhibition. As Kathy Munro, honorary associate professor in the School of Architecture and Planning at Wits and chair of the Johannesburg Heritage Foundation explains, 'The Tower of Light is a rare treasure of international significance; it is iconic in its architectural language, its expression of modernity for the time and in its functionality.'[9] The Tower of Light was designed by the then Wits professor of architecture Geoffrey Pearce, and still exists as part of the redeveloped Braamfontein Campus West. It was an anchor point for the

Diagrammatic plan of the Rand Showgrounds between 1912 and 1924. This is the design that won the 'lay-out competition'. Source: University of the Witwatersrand's Central Records Office and Archives

cableway that carried people from Victory Avenue, down the hill, towards Empire Road. It was also the show-time studio for LM Radio and Springbok Radio.

The Braamfontein Campus West was not always an uncontested space. The Braamfontein Campus East had to endure the huge influx of traffic and people to their neighbourhood when the Rand Show was held, and in fact organised the student calendar so that holidays would fall during the dates when it was held. The West Campus became infamous in 1960 for the attempted assassination of the then prime minister Hendrik Verwoerd, as he opened the show in the aftermath of the Sharpeville anti-apartheid uprising and massacre. Verwoerd was shot in the face by David Pratt, a member of the Agricultural Society, but survived.

BUILDING NEW SPACES

The influence of the University's Faculty of Architecture on both the theory and practice of the built infrastructure of the growing city of Johannesburg was significant. Before the Second World War, the faculty was one of the centres of colonial modernism, the international style that had spread throughout Europe in the early decades of the century. Critical to the faculty's impact were the influence and networks of Wits academic Professor Rex Martienssen, himself an early student in the department (BArch 1930, MArch 1940 and DLitt 1941). He became an associate of the Royal Institute of British Architects in 1930 and in 1939 was elected president of the Transvaal Institute of Architects.

Photograph of the Tower of Light, taken by Dennis Adams. Source: University of the Witwatersrand's Central Records Office and Archives

Exterior of the John Moffat Building and the pond located on the Wits Braamfontein Campus East. Photo: Sally Gaule

Martienssen became a senior lecturer in architecture at Wits and travelled to Europe frequently to stay abreast of changes and current trends. While abroad in 1934, he met the legendary architect, urban planner and theorist of modernism, Le Corbusier, which was the start of an enduring friendship. That year, Martienssen established a private practice in Johannesburg, and designed his own home, House Martienssen in Greenside, based on international modernist principles – a house quite remarkable even by current standards. It was one of a small number of Le Corbusier-inspired houses built in South Africa in the 1930s. Others were House Munro in Pretoria by McIntosh in 1932, House Harris in Houghton by Hanson, Tomkin and Finkelstein in 1933, and, the best example, House Stern in Johannesburg, built by Martienssen and his partners Fassler and Cooke in 1934. Martienssen was married to fellow architect and art historian Professor Heather Martienssen, who became the first female professor at Wits – in fine arts – and who for decades gave her name to the prize for the best fine arts student at Wits.

The Rex Martienssen House in Greenside, Johannesburg. Forerunner of the modernist architecture movement in South Africa and former Wits lecturer, Professor Rex Martienssen died at the age of 37 while in training with the South African Air Force during the Second World War. Photo: Daniel Born

In 1959 the Faculty of Architecture and the Department of Fine Arts had moved to a home of their own on the Braamfontein Campus East, to a new building designed by Professor John Fassler of the University's Department of Architecture. This was the first of the buildings to be completed in the University's post-war building programme. It was named the John Moffat Building, a tribute to the Johannesburg architect who died in 1941, and who donated some £100 000 to the University on condition that the funds be used for a building. The John Moffat Building was a notable addition to the University's facilities for teaching and study, comparable environmentally and architecturally to buildings of a similar nature and purpose at universities throughout the Western world.

OUTER SPACE IS HERE

One of the most recognisable spaces at Wits, and one with which the public readily identifies, is the Planetarium. It opened on 12 October 1960 – the first planetarium in Africa and only the second in the Southern Hemisphere. The idea of setting up a planetarium was first discussed in 1956 when the Johannesburg Festival Committee – instituted to organise the celebrations of the City's 70th anniversary – decided to raise funds to buy and house a Zeiss planetarium projector for the celebrations. With little time to obtain a new instrument, it was decided to buy an existing planetarium projector from Europe. After lengthy negotiations, the committee succeeded in persuading the parliament of Hamburg to sell their planetarium's projector, which had been in use since 1930. Soon, the responsibilities of the committee were taken over by the Johannesburg City Council, which, after further negotiations, sold the projector to Wits for use as both an academic facility for the instruction of students and as a public amenity. Plans for a new building to house the projector were drawn up in 1958, construction began in 1959 and the Planetarium was opened in 1960. It is still a thriving educational institution for the general public today, although the magnificent but antiquated Zeiss projection system is being upgraded.

The Wits Digital Dome, a major centenary project, is set to transform the Planetarium into an interdisciplinary, state-of-the-art data science exploration and discovery facility. It will straddle diverse fields, from radio astronomy and fluid dynamics to anatomy and lightning studies, from science exploration to the digital arts. This will provide a unique resource for both Wits staff and students, and will also benefit school learners and the broader public.

UNIQUE EDUCATIONAL PLACES

The Adler Museum of Medicine, the only one of its kind in South Africa and one of the most comprehensive medical history museums in the world, was founded in 1962 by Drs Cyril and Esther Adler and was handed over to Wits University in 1974. Cyril Adler graduated from Wits and his wife was the long-term custodian of the museum and collection, which started life in a flat owned by the then School of Medicine, and which moved around the City as it outgrew its premises. It now has a permanent home in the Wits Faculty of Health Sciences in Parktown.

The Adlers assembled a remarkable private collection of medical and pharmacological memorabilia of over 40 000 objects depicting the history of medicine, dentistry and pharmacy. Apart from the items of medical historical interest on display, there are also documents, sculptures, pictures, videos, and philatelic and medallion collections relating to medical history. The museum also has a library of rare books and a medical history reference library.

An important focus for the museum is the practice of traditional medicine in Africa, showcased through displays of an African herb shop and a patient consulting a *sangoma* (traditional medicine practitioner). The museum, like the Planetarium, is a fitting example of the connection between the University and its communities in the city at

Students relax outside the Commerce Library, with the Tower of Light in the background.
Photo: Shivan Parusnath

SPACE AND PLACE

Visitors to the Wits Adler Museum of Medicine are provided with a glimpse into the history of medicine and dentistry in South Africa through the rare books and exhibits on display. Photo: Daniel Born

Close-up of one of the early ear syringes used in medicine on display at the Wits Adler Museum of Medicine. Photo: Daniel Born

large, offering regular public lectures, tours, specialised tours for school learners, film shows and temporary exhibitions on various subjects. It also provides excellent facilities for medical historical teaching and research.

A CORNER OF ITS OWN

Wits is undeniably a city university, embedded in Braamfontein and Parktown. 'Braam', a trendy, vibrant inner-city hub, is known for its food and fashion districts, its art and entertainment offerings, its social justice organisations, and the many retail stores that serve young people. 'There is probably no better place in the real world to "get that Wakanda feeling" than the campus of the University of the Witwatersrand (Wits) in Johannesburg,' the Associated Press said in 2018. 'To be surrounded by smart, opinionated, articulate students, fashionably dressed in colourful, sharp clothes, full of hope and plans for themselves, their country and their continent is to feel the heart of the Afro-optimism of "Black Panther",' wrote the American news agency's Andrew Meldrum.[10]

One of the dominant landmarks in Braamfontein has belonged to Wits since the 1970s. University Corner, on the corner of Bertha and Jorissen streets, and which now houses the Wits Art Museum, Wits Journalism, Wits Press, the Gauteng City-Region Observatory, Drama for Life, music studios and other Wits entities, was once a service station and dealership that belonged to local entrepreneur and property developer Wilfred Lawson. His garage – complete with street frontage onto Jan Smuts Avenue – was eventually developed into a 21-storey skyscraper, topped by one of the most recognisable landmarks in the city: a revolving restaurant and nightclub resembling a flying saucer!

The revolving restaurant on top of University Corner flanked by the Wits School of Arts. Photo: Daniel Born

This particular corner of the University's city-facing spaces was redeveloped in 2012 and forms part of Johannesburg's cultural arc, which starts in Newtown, sweeps through Braamfontein and ends at Constitution Hill. The prominent and successful Wits Art Museum, which houses over 15 000 works of art, was opened in 2012, when Wits turned 90. The Wits School of Arts building is being revamped, and the new Chris Seabrooke Music Hall, a centenary project, was opened in 2022.

Directly across Jan Smuts Avenue was Lawson's other major 1970s investment building, Noswal Hall ('Lawson' spelled backwards). The ground floor of this office block housed Street Records, a cult record shop and vinyl library and a student staple of the late 1970s and 1980s. Later, the building was converted into student accommodation and is today part of Wits' Braamfontein Residence Cluster.

The arty character of University Corner has an earlier precedent. Herbert Prins, at the time a lecturer in the Department of Architecture, tells the story of how the landmark Nunnery Theatre came to be. The Department of Dramatic Art was scheduled to open in 1971. With the opening imminent, Prins was visited by two lecturers, somewhat in a panic. John van Zyl and Art de Villiers were more than a little concerned. Calamity – they still didn't have a performance venue! Although the University had provided the hall next to the Catholic church for use, it still needed to be redesigned and converted, and only a minuscule budget was available.

'It so happened,' says Prins, 'that Malcolm Purkey, who later became a professor in the Department of Dramatic Art and director of the Market Theatre, was a student in the department. He came to me and said that he was interested to help with the conversion of

The Nunnery in 2020. Photo: Daniel Born

The former service station and dealership was redeveloped in 2012, and the University's city-facing space was developed into what is now the prominent and successful Wits Art Museum. Source: Wits Art Museum

the space. I then approached various building suppliers and obtained scaffolding at no charge and glulam timber at a reduced price. Malcolm and I met on a Saturday morning and gathered a gang of casual workers and enthusiastic student helpers and set to work, finishing the next day!'[11] Staff and students used this temporary structure for over 50 years.

More recently the areas around The Nunnery have been upgraded – the Wits School of Arts building has been revamped and a new state-of-the-art Music Hall has been established. The purpose-built Wits Chris Seabrooke Music Hall is a magnificent, intimate setting with acoustics and facilities to present professional-quality music performances across multiple genres. Adjacent to the Wits Art Museum and the new Digital Arts building, it is a propitious addition to the burgeoning Wits Cultural Precinct. In

*Collage of images on the construction of the Braamfontein Roman Catholic Church, from beginning to completion. Its church hall was transformed into the Department of Dramatic Art's first performance venue, The Nunnery.
Source: University of the Witwatersrand's Central Records Office and Archives*

addition to providing a handsome venue for student performances, it contributes a deeply valued cultural resource to the City.

The Wits Theatre Complex, opposite The Nunnery, opened its doors in July 1983. The plans for the theatre were first announced ten years before and money was raised from the public and private sectors (the complex cost in the region of R5 million). The old Dental Hospital opposite The Nunnery became the new location for the consolidated School of Arts. Today the Wits School of Arts positions itself strongly as an urban, African and global school, and has produced some prominent graduates, staff and alumni, including musician James Phillips, artist William Kentridge, screenwriter and actor Gavin Hood, and pianist Anton Nel. Professor Jeanne Zaidel-Rudolph from the Wits School of Arts was the first woman to attain her doctorate in music composition in South Africa and was responsible for the composite version of South Africa's current national multi-language anthem. The national anthem sub-national committee was chaired by Wits Professor of African Languages Mzilikazi Khumalo, and included Richard Cock, Fatima Meer, Zaidel-Rudolph and others. The school is located within the Faculty of Humanities, which is renowned for its academic rigour, research excellence and commitment to social justice. The faculty consistently ranks as the best humanities faculty on the continent.

CONTESTED SPACES

Senate House, the main administrative building of the University, was opened in 1977. Like the John Moffat Building, it was designed by Professor John Fassler. Adjacent to the Braamfontein-facing buildings on the corner of Jan Smuts Avenue, it was designed in the brutalist style – in contrast to the neo-classical language employed in the early major buildings of the University, including the Wits Great Hall.

Senate House serves as the administration block of Wits, and since it is built around a central concourse that once doubled up as a student canteen, it has always been a focal point and rallying space for student protests and political organisation. This was the case right through the apartheid era and during the #FeesMustFall protests. In the wake of #FeesMustFall, the Students' Representative Council made a formal request to the Wits Naming Committee to rename the block Solomon Mahlangu House, which was granted. The official name change came into effect in 2016, thus memorialising Solomon Mahlangu (1956–1979), the Mamelodi High School student who joined the ANC in 1976 and who went into exile to receive military training. His bravery as a student activist resonated strongly with contemporary students, who sought to honour his memory and legacy of struggle. Mahlangu had been apprehended when re-entering South Africa, was convicted of murder under the 'common purpose' law, and was tried and then hanged at Pretoria Central Prison on 6 April 1979.

Wits is indelibly etched into the fabric of Johannesburg. The University has developed a living legacy beyond its buildings and infrastructure, and has continued an illustrious history of turning spaces into inhabited places for its people to grow, develop, create, and advance the public good.

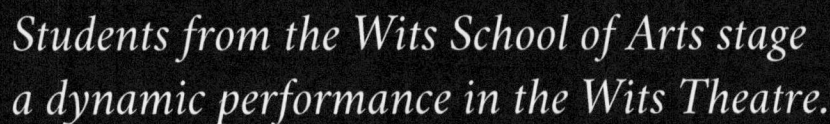

Students from the Wits School of Arts stage a dynamic performance in the Wits Theatre.
Photo: Sally Gaule

90% OF THE WEALTH IS OWNED BY 10% OF THE POPULATION! THEY MUST PAY FOR OUR
ENOUGH MONEY FOR THE WORLD CUP ENOUGH MONEY FOR COMMONWEALTH GAMES NO MONEY FOR EDUCATION?
NATIONALISE UNDER WORKER CONTROL
#HABIBISM – FORCED MILITARISED EDUCATION!

WE LEAD CHANGE

Behind the Scenes of #FeesMustFall

On 14 October 2015, South Africa's newspaper headlines led with the story that students at Wits University had disrupted classes, shut down the campus and occupied the administration building. The following Monday, students at 20 of the then 23 universities across the country embarked on similar action. How did the movement go from a Wits University student protest to a national event that changed the course of South Africa's history?

Some of the thousands of #FeesMustFall protesters who marched to the Union Buildings in Pretoria calling for free tertiary education in October 2015. Photo: Alon Skuy

Wits students Shaeera Kalla, Mcebo Dlamini, Nompendulo Mkhatshwa and Fasiha Hassan were the leaders of the #FeesMustFall student protests during 2015. It all began after the Wits Council, plagued by declining state subsidy and income, resolved to raise tuition fees for 2016 by 10.5%, a move that the Students' Representative Council (SRC) feared would be unaffordable for many students. The students had three seats on the Wits Council, and despite their objecting to the proposed fee increase, the vote was lost.

Although they still felt very strongly about the way forward, the SRC realised that they had exhausted all available options. 'We took to the streets because we had no other choice,' explains Fasiha Hassan. The protest was the ultimate alternative.

SPACE AND PLACE

In early October 2015, a Wits Workers' Solidarity Committee initiative termed the 'October 6 movement' was formed, calling for the insourcing of workers at Wits. Coupled with the objection to the proposed fee increments, this mass mobilisation brought together academics, students and workers in support of a common cause – access to quality, decolonised higher education for all.

Hassan describes with pride the series of events that led to a national movement in the interests of free education. The SRC held a brainstorming meeting to discuss a protest and the students divided themselves into sub-committees segmented into research, mobilisation and media. The result was an extremely well-organised, peaceful protest, which was truly a 'moment of innovation' for the Wits students who were determined to do it differently this time, owing to the urgency and importance of the matter. Ordinarily, student protests consisted of singing struggle songs, handing over a memorandum and then waiting for a result. The students felt that if the doors of learning were to be closed to all, everyone would be unable to access education and

Students gathered in the Senate House concourse in 2015 to discuss their grievances. Photo: Lauren Mulligan

'Wits is the epicentre, ground zero, and the place that determines the future of the country.' Fasiha Hassan

everyone would be inconvenienced, angry and upset. And so the idea of a shutdown, to quite literally 'close the gates', was born.

The academic programme was the main bargaining chip that the students had to negotiate.

Very early on the morning of Wednesday, 14 October 2015, their parents unaware of what lay ahead on that fateful day, several brave young activists left home. They hoped that their flyers calling for students to join in a midday march to Senate House (now Solomon Mahlangu House) would achieve the desired effect. By 6 am, the students were seated in front of the University's entrance gates on Empire Road and Jorissen Street and at the entrance of the Flower Hall. Fasiha Hassan, who was later awarded the Norwegian Student Peace Prize for her role in the #FeesMustFall movement, recalls that time: 'Our convictions were tested, we really had to believe in what we were doing.' By the end of the day, the group had swelled to a few hundred, the original six students having been joined by other anxious students who had their own concerns about how they were going to pay their university fees.

By the following day, a few thousand students were supporting the call for affordable education. On Friday, 16 October 2015, the

SPACE AND PLACE

Wits students and academics protesting on campus during #FeesMustFall. Source: University of the Witwatersrand's Central Records Office and Archives

third day of the protest, student leaders from universities across the country expressed their wish to join the movement. By the time the country woke up the next Monday, the protest had taken on an organic life and grown into a national movement. It was no longer just about Wits. 'Wits led these changes not only for their students but to serve a national agenda, that of giving students agency and a voice,' says Hassan.

What began as #WitsProtest soon faded when the student leaders realised that it was unclear to anyone on social media what the protest was about. Initially, they changed their hashtag to #WitsFeesProtest, before realising that this was too long for social media. The students were in agreement that the word 'fees' had to be in the title, and 'fall' was included because of the momentum of the #RhodesMustFall campaign, a transformation campaign that had started at the University of Cape Town earlier that year. Much debate followed over the inclusion of the word 'must', but eventually the leaders settled on it, agreeing that it conveyed a sense of determination. And so, out of a need for a definite outcome, #FeesMustFall was born.

While the protests lasted over two years, the movement experienced peaks and troughs, mainly because it was difficult to sustain momentum over such a long period of time, Hassan explains. The positive outcome that the students were looking for finally came in December 2017, when Jacob Zuma, the then president of South Africa, made an announcement in which he committed to provide free tertiary education to students whose household income was less than R600 000 per annum. While this did force a major policy change, it has not yet solved the problem of the 'missing middle' – those students who do not qualify for financial aid from the state, and who cannot afford to pay their own way.

Wits is now exploring alternative ways to raise funds for student endowments for talented students who fall into this category.

Fasiha Hassan is a proud Witsie and is even prouder of what she and her peers managed to achieve in their early 20s when they changed the course of history. 'I would not have taken on this fight if I wasn't at Wits,' she maintains, then adds: 'I would not have had the courage if it wasn't for being conscientised at Wits.' She is of the belief that 'Wits is the epicentre, ground zero, and the place that determines the future of the country'. She explains further: 'It is a microcosm of society. The role of the university is to set the tone and be innovative in terms of the politics of the country, together with science and technology. Wits' legacy to be innovative and change society will outlive us all.'

There was a sense of community coming together when people sustained the protesters with donations of food and water, and fifth- and sixth-year medical students assisted protesters requiring first aid. Umrabulo[12] was also in service, with postgraduate students providing tutorials and study sessions between 4 pm and 6 pm daily so that students did not fall behind with their studies.

Wits is home to a large number of 'missing-middle' students, and in 2022 administered over R1 billion in financial aid, scholarships and bursaries that benefit about 65 per cent of its student population.

Wits alumnus Maurice Smithers on a busy street in Yeoville. Photo: Daniel Born

ACTIVISTS, SCIENTISTS AND A LIFETIME OF SERVICE: MAURICE SMITHERS

Failing Forward

It might be just four years younger than Johannesburg, but the suburb of Yeoville proves that planning and architecture are not just about designing cities, streets and buildings. Structures and spaces can in fact shape societies and cultures.

The once quiet urban village mushroomed into a bustling nightlife hotspot in the late 1970s. Artists and activists moved into the area and Rockey Street, the main drag, reverberated with the sounds of jazz clubs, rock 'n' roll performances and theatre productions.

Today the small suburb has been reinvented. Visit the local market and you'll be greeted with a smorgasbord of smells from bubbling pots of Zimbabwean stews, Congolese cassava and Ethiopian curries.

Maurice Smithers knows this changing shape and cultural shift better than anyone. He has dedicated many years of his life to community development in Yeoville and neighbouring Bellevue by trying to understand the space, its needs and its people. He moved there in the 1970s – after dropping out of a BA programme at Wits – to join several like-minded activists in the fight against apartheid.

'My dream for Yeoville-Bellevue is that it will become a cultural tourism destination, where different cultures are celebrated.' Maurice Smithers

After 1994, the face of the neighbourhood began changing. In 1991, 85 per cent of Yeoville-Bellevue residents were white. By 1998, over 90 per cent were Black. Yet dignity and social justice remained a distant hope for many residents because of a lack of meaningful transformation and planning. Communal spaces began falling into disrepair. Economic opportunities plummeted.

Smithers became what he calls a 'resident activist'. 'I wanted to make a difference in the way in which my neighbourhood functioned,' he explains.

Working with other activists, he set out to address issues like urban decay, socio-economic challenges and social discord in the area. In his 15 years in this role, there were several successes but also a slew of frustrations – and even threats against him and his family from community members running under-the-counter operations. 'Still, our organisation persuaded the Johannesburg Development Agency to fix the local pool, build a library and clean up the park, amongst other improvements,' Smithers says. 'In 2008 I convinced them to give me a salary for a year so I could work full-time in the community.'

He resigned from a well-paying job in the provincial government to create the Yeoville-Bellevue Community Development Trust. One of his proudest achievements was helping to create a culture of appreciation for Yeoville-Bellevue's pan-Africanism. 'In May 2010, with a grant from the City of Johannesburg, we held the first-ever Africa Day Carnival and Festival to celebrate the pan-African nature of the area. It was fantastic – we closed off the streets and had six stages.'

That same year, Yeoville Studio saw the light – a research and teaching initiative representing a collaboration between civil society and the Wits School of Architecture and Planning. Smithers worked closely with the studio's strategic team. 'The aim was for students to engage with the community and so become better planners. The studio generated a rich archive of research proposing innovative, community-oriented interventions in its two years.'

Even though he moved to Kensington in 2015, Smithers says that he is not done in Yeoville-Bellevue. 'My dream for the area is that it will become a cultural tourism destination, where different cultures are not only celebrated but can help form the basis for an economic revival.'

Smithers re-enrolled at Wits in 2017, at the age of 66, to complete his master's in development planning, producing a paper that explored the interface between liquor licensing and municipal planning. Today, he is the director of the Southern African Alcohol Policy Alliance.

Smithers wrote a book detailing his 15 years of neighbourhood development work. Re-imagining Post-Apartheid Yeoville Bellevue: The Journey and Reflections of a Resident-Activist/Activist-Resident *was published in 2013 by the South African Research Chair in Development Planning and Modelling in the Wits School of Architecture and Planning.*

WE HARNESS THE POWER OF PLACE

Wits Rural Campus: The Hidden Gem

In stark contrast to its counterpart in gritty, urbanised Johannesburg, the Wits Rural Campus (WRC) is surrounded by open spaces where herds of antelope roam amongst marula trees. Visitors are warned to avoid walking or jogging on the property between dusk and dawn. This is when an elusive leopard trawls the 350-hectare bushveld estate near Bushbuckridge on the border of Limpopo, Mpumalanga and Mozambique, some 500 kilometres from Johannesburg.

The Wits Rural Campus is truly interdisciplinary, serving as a base that enables Wits researchers and students from a range of disciplines to engage with rural issues in a wider development context. Photo: Lisa Marie Albert

WORLD-CLASS RESEARCH BASE

Despite its tranquil rural setting – or perhaps because of it – the campus is a world-class research base that hosts some of Wits' longest-running and most impactful studies.

Professor John Gear's vision to establish a multidisciplinary rural teaching and research facility in the 1980s was in response to the critique that Wits was essentially an urban university. Professor Gear argued that 'rural and urban are two sides of the same coin. The fate of one impacts the other.'

Over a third of South Africans live in rural settings today, including more than half of South Africa's poor. 'When the WRC had its beginnings in 1989, the great majority of the population lived in rural areas and were vulnerable to many health and environmental

The Wits Rural Campus has enabled impactful interdisciplinary research, student training and community engagement in rural Bushbuckridge for 33 years. Photo: Graham Delacy

risks,' says Professor Stephen Tollman, co-founder and director of the Medical Research Council/Wits Rural Public Health and Health Transitions Research Unit (known colloquially as Agincourt, the name of the village and sub-district where field activities are centred). 'It was unconscionable to us that research resources were primarily located in the country's urban centres, and not where the need was greatest. We wanted to contribute through making a meaningful impact in rural South Africa.'

Professor Tollman and Professor Kathleen Kahn, his life partner and Agincourt co-founder and senior scientist, lived at Tintswalo Hospital near the WRC for much of the 1990s while establishing Agincourt. Today, it is one of the longest-running population-based research centres on the continent. The research infrastructure is located at Tintswalo Hospital, near Agincourt village (40 kilometres from the WRC) under the auspices of the School of Public Health at Wits in Johannesburg. 'We aimed to help realign health systems to be more equitable. As we did that, we realised that there were not adequate information systems for rational and evidence-based decision making. So we set out to put them in place,' says Kahn.

A monumental task lay ahead: getting consent from and engaging every resident in 31 identified villages in the area, to establish a system to generate data over the long term. 'At that point, estimates showed 30 000 people living in the area,' says Tollman. 'We counted 70 000, in this extremely rural setting with no hospital or even a small town in sight.'

COMMUNITY DEVELOPMENT
After more than 25 years of annually recording every birth and death, migration, education, union, socio-economic status and health issue in the community, now some 120 000 people strong, Agincourt has generated invaluable data. The observational and intervention studies enable researchers to identify trends in socio-economic status, inequality amongst communities, rapidly changing mortality and migration patterns, and the impact of infectious and non-communicable diseases on already strained health and social systems. 'Our work informs healthcare policy on chronic conditions, HIV prevention and mental healthcare,' says Kahn. 'It influences the distribution of social grants, and has global impact via the World Health Organization, international NGOs and research partnerships.'

Agincourt can accommodate nearly 300 people in its guest houses, flatlets and en suite rooms, dormitories and student research camps. It is also open to the public. Facilities include two swimming pools, a restaurant and catering services, and a network of roads for walking and jogging. Staff and students have access to a computer laboratory, data and Wi-Fi facilities, a wet and dry laboratory, staff housing, and office space.

The granite Lowveld savanna vegetation provides a habitat for a range of wildlife, including giraffe, blue wildebeest, Burchell's zebra, kudu, waterbuck, impala, reedbuck, bushbuck, grey duiker, warthog, chacma baboon, vervet monkey and several mongoose species. Nocturnal species such as bush pig, aardvark, pangolin, porcupine, civet, small spotted genet, thick-tailed bushbaby and lesser bushbaby can also be observed. Small predators include caracal and serval. Over 180 bird species have been recorded on the property.

Another unique aspect is the potential for comparing public health research in rural and urban settings, using longitudinal studies. The data generated via Agincourt in a rural setting over three decades can be studied and compared with the Birth to Twenty programme based in Soweto, the largest and longest-running study of children's health and development in Africa, and one of the few large-scale longitudinal studies in the world.

SPACE AND PLACE

An exemplar of what universities need to do to change society for the better, Wits Rural Campus provides a bridge between rich and poor, rural and urban, and local and international. Source: University of the Witwatersrand's Central Records Office and Archives

Ongoing interdisciplinary research happens in collaboration with scientists on the continent and in Southeast Asia, the UK, USA and Europe. This research approach provides a base to mentor new generations of early- and mid-career scientists in several fields – supporting career paths that are difficult to navigate alone.

'In the beginning, we were determined to prove everyone wrong who said that establishing a world-class platform for health and development in a remote setting would be difficult. We knew that our research had to be outstanding to achieve this platform, and community engagement has been just as important,' says Tollman.

This continuous commitment to community development has ensured critical health interventions, and facilitated economic and capacity-building opportunities, adds Kahn. 'Over the years, we have employed thousands of staff from the villages, and trained them as fieldworkers, counsellors, project managers or data technicians. We committed to these communities and I believe that we're fulfilling that commitment.'

'It was unconscionable to us that research resources were primarily located in the country's urban centres, and not where the need was greatest.'
Professor Stephen Tollman

SUSTAINABLE FUTURE

Professor Wayne Twine from the School of Animal, Plant and Environmental Sciences has lived on the property with his family for more than 20 years. He heads up the campus's other long-term research programme, called SUNRAE (Sustaining Natural Resources in African Ecosystems). 'The programme focuses on the human dimension of resource conservation, from livelihoods and food security to sustaining natural resources and weathering environmental changes,' he says.

Sustainability in rural areas, Twine explains, is not just an environmental issue, but also a human one. 'Though 90 per cent of households in the area have electricity, 60 per cent still rely on natural resources because they can't afford electricity or appliances. The environment delivers essential services to these families, including water, firewood, food and medicinal herbs.'

Some studies under the SUNRAE programme have focused on understanding what needs to change to make these resources more sustainable. Twine gives an example: 'One PhD student assessed the feasibility of the community-based management of the rotational harvesting of coppice [resprouting shoots] to increase wood production to sustainably meet the local demand.'

Twine is also the director of the Wits Rural Knowledge Hub, which was established in 2013 to integrate, synthesise and share research. 'The campus really is a remarkable asset to the University,' he says proudly, 'since most southern institutions don't have the resources to run rural facilities. Those that exist in the Global South are often operated by northern institutions or are focused exclusively on agriculture or environmental sciences. The Wits Rural Campus is truly interdisciplinary, serving as a base that enables Wits researchers and students from a range of disciplines to engage with rural issues in a wider development context.

'It's essential to do this type of work in South Africa, which is both a rural and an urban country. There exists this false dichotomy that rural and urban living are separate systems. In our country they are intimately linked – for example, around 60 per cent of adult males from the area work in urban areas and send money home. The challenge is to ensure that our science translates to positive societal change. The impact of our work is evidence that we are making very good progress.'

'The Wits Rural Campus is part of Wits University's fundamental agenda and is an exemplar of what universities need to do to change society for the better. We are a bridge between rich and poor, rural and urban, local and international, and a link between different countries and communities.' Professor Adam Habib[13]

WE CREATE AND APPLY KNOWLEDGE

Knowing Your Place

The Global Change Institute (GCI) at Wits University puts a unique perspective on the phrase 'knowing your place'. The GCI is a continental leader in climate-change science that takes knowledge, research and insights about our changing world into policy, civil society and the business sector. As such, the GCI embraces a transdisciplinary approach, where skills from many different academic disciplines and sources of knowledge are integrated to create sustainable solutions with (as opposed to for) its partners in society.

Climate change causes extreme weather patterns such as droughts, flash floods and soaring temperatures. Land degradation from poor development practice is an additional stressor in African landscapes. Together, the impacts threaten all living organisms. Photo: Barend Erasmus

This synergy between academia, industry and government makes noteworthy contributions to risk mitigation, good governance and the generation of sustainable strategies.

The GCI runs world-class climate models that can pinpoint future climate changes at scales relevant to local decision-making, along with the unique insights that come from being deeply embedded in the African environment. Professor Francois Engelbrecht, a climatologist at the GCI, offers insight into the findings of a group of UK scientists, who determined that a total of 28 trillion tonnes of ice have melted over the past 23 years and who estimate that this will cause sea levels to rise by a total of one metre by the end of the century.

Alexandra in Johannesburg experiences flooding every year due to homes being built beside the Jukskei River. Photo: Daniel Born

'Climate science itself should increasingly be used as an adaptation tool towards anticipating regional tipping points in the African climate system.' Professor Francois Engelbrecht[14]

To understand the volume of 28 trillion tonnes of ice, Engelbrecht gives a graphic example and an explanation: 'It is the equivalent of a metre-deep area covering the Free State and the North West provinces in South Africa. The melting of this tremendous amount of ice comes as a consequence of our reliance on burning fossil fuels for energy.'

The institute is well placed to understand the ecosystems, constraints and capabilities of the local environment. The late Distinguished Professor Bob Scholes (1957–2021), an A-rated scientist and former director of the GCI, put it simply: 'We grew up here,' he said. 'This is our home.'

REIMAGINING URBAN ENVIRONMENTS

Wits University and the City of Johannesburg have formed a partnership aimed at co-generating solutions on issues of urbanisation, migration and green buildings. The GCI hosts multiple programmes where scholars from all over Africa collaborate to imagine urban environments of the future.

Some of the responsibilities of navigating the challenges of the twenty-first century in South Africa lie with government, in setting policy, passing legislation and imposing appropriate regulations. The GCI is able to assist government with this task through the scientific assessments of issues that are technically complicated but of high social impact. Climate change is one such problem; the potential development of shale gas resources in the Karoo through fracking is another.

'Globally and locally we are confronted by environmental thresholds. We need to be aware that our water and food security systems are at risk and that this has vast implications for the wellbeing of people and the planet.' Professor Coleen Vogel

A well-considered decision requires input from technical experts such as climatologists, ecologists and engineers – but also from economists, social scientists, lawyers and historians. Since a strong ethical dimension is frequently involved, the choices may need to be guided by philosophers and anthropologists. Often, the social acceptability of developments involves notions such as 'sense of place', which may be best approached by listening to poets, artists and indigenous communities.

A collaboration between artist Hannelie Coetzee and Wits ecologist Professor Sally Archibald culminated in a large-scale ecological artwork, which took place in the Khatlhampi Private Reserve. Titled Eland and Benko, it featured the image of a little boy reaching out to touch an eland. The work brought together scientific exploration and artistic expression as well as human and non-human experience. Photo: Shivan Parusnath

Aerial view of the remarkable Working on Fire project. The artwork of figures etched into the hillside, titled *Locust and Grasshopper*, aimed to improve the management of grasslands in conservation areas and to highlight the importance of creating more diverse and productive grasslands.

Photo: Shivan Parusnath

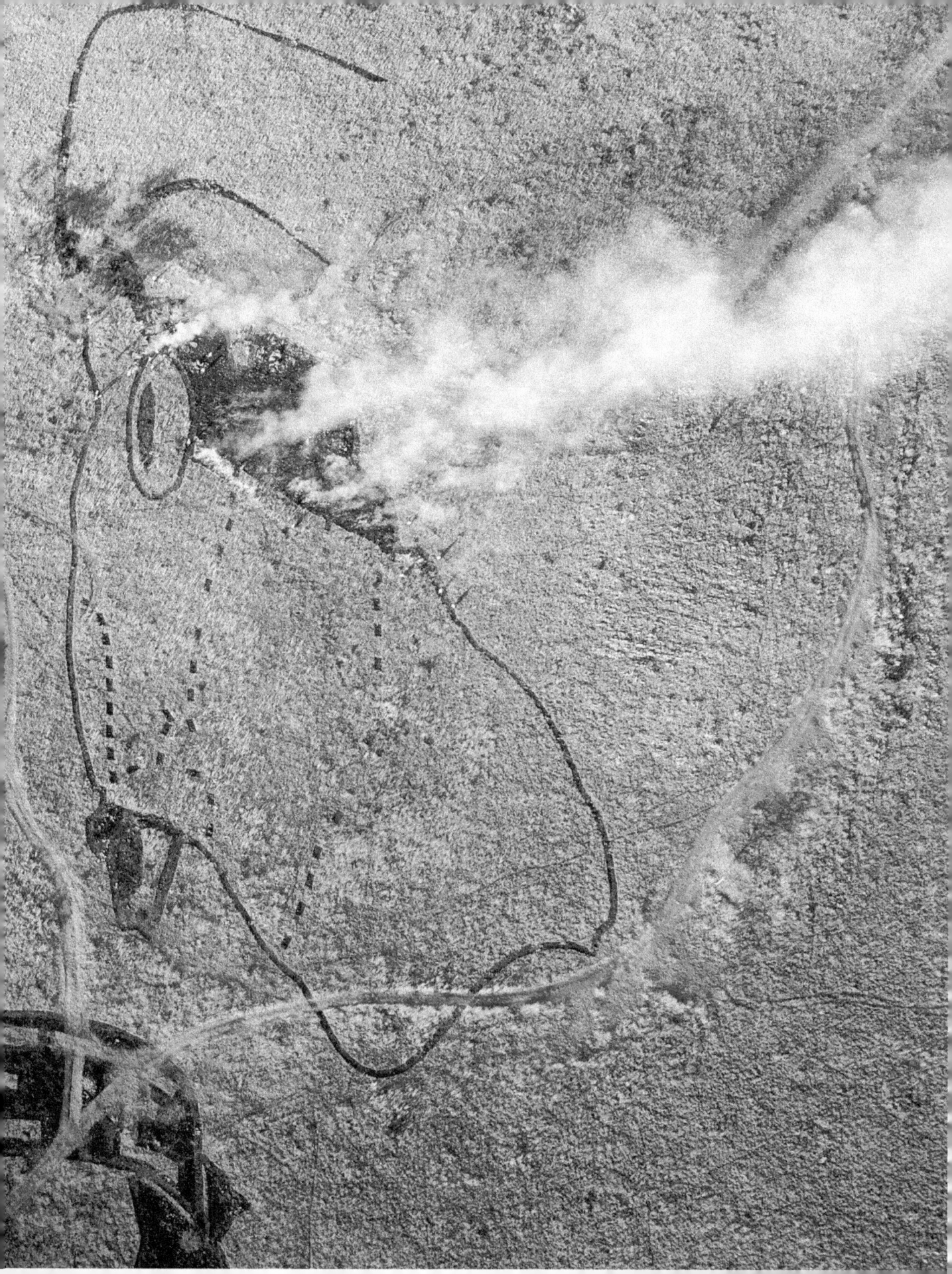

Wits embraces the notion that the engine of human creativity is cities. An urban future need not be a dystopia; we can mould the future that we want. Most African cities are yet to be built. Once established, they keep their form for centuries. So, setting off on the right path initially is crucially important, and within our grasp.

As Scholes said: 'We need to be more open and transparent in our conversations and respect each other's points of view.'

The GCI is also leaving its mark globally. Many on the GCI team have participated in the Intergovernmental Panel on Climate Change (IPCC) and the Intergovernmental Platform on Biodiversity and Ecosystem Services. 'Our sense of place,' said Scholes, 'is not just our immediate proximity but encompasses how what happens in Africa affects the world and is affected by it. For this reason, we collaborate with organisations worldwide.'

Scholes shared some of the insights from a GCI report titled *The Climate Risks We Face in the 21st Century*, where a 'top five' list of interactive risk clusters and consequences is set to challenge the realities of South Africans. This authoritative reference document highlights top-rated risk factors, including food insecurity and the viability of the agricultural sector; shortages of clean water; a poorly handled transition to low-carbon energy, heat stress and disrupted ecosystems; and loss of biodiversity. All the risk factors feed into one another, thereby effectively working as 'threat multipliers'.

GENERATIONS OF CLIMATE SCIENCE EXCELLENCE AT WITS

Wits Professor Stanley Jackson was the former doyen of African climate studies. His enormous *Climatological Atlas of Africa*, first published in the 1960s, guided the continent's agricultural and water resource development. It also established Wits as a reputable place to study climatology.

The baton was taken up by Professor Peter Tyson, a world-leading climatologist and a former deputy vice-chancellor of the University. He was one of the founders of the International Geosphere-Biosphere Programme, which, in the 1990s, built our current understanding of human-caused climate change.

This tradition continues with Professors Francois Engelbrecht and Coleen Vogel, both distinguished professors at the GCI, and Dr Laura Pereira, all of whom specialise in climate-related issues. If we want to save the world by finding solutions to the most important challenges of our time, we will need not only technical excellence but also participatory, listening and narrative skills. This is what the GCI strives to offer its growing cohort of master's and PhD students and postdoctoral fellows.

A HOPEFUL FUTURE

The GCI regards the movement of people from rural to urban areas not as a tide to be stemmed, but as an opportunity to redesign the future. Urbanisation provides opportunities to create liveable environments that have a positive impact on the planet. 'I am interested in the human side of climate change – how we can adapt and make ourselves more resilient in the face of climate change,' says Vogel. 'Globally and locally we are confronted by environmental thresholds. We need to be aware that our water and food security systems are at risk and that this has vast implications for the wellbeing of people and the planet.'

A world leader in climate science, Vogel is one of the key authors of a series of global assessments for the IPCC. She has chaired a range of international committees and serves on a number of international boards, including the African science committee of Future Earth.

'I have been fortunate that my research and position have enabled me to assist and collaborate with various actors, including governments and organisations worldwide, to grapple with making the decisions required for a sustainable future. This has also enabled me to do transdisciplinary research at an international level, not only between the physical and social sciences, but also to better understand how we can engage the wider public, society and business to make decisions around climate change.'

As a distinguished professor, Vogel is focusing on Africa, including creating a cohort of young academics who can best work on climate-change themes. Vogel has developed a considerable number of PhD students who are now sitting in positions of authority in government and a wide range of sectors in South Africa and internationally.

'We grew up here. This is our home.'
Professor Bob Scholes

The late Distinguished Professor Bob Scholes.
Photo: Eyescape Photography

'I hope that I have enabled them to be critical in their positions and to make critical decisions,' she says. 'In my current position I want to continue developing the next generation of scholars, particularly women, to take their place in the climate-change field.'

There is a need to rethink our relationship with the environment, in both urban and rural areas, and pose useful questions that require solutions. For example, can Johannesburg thrive on the water it receives from rainfall, or must it import water from distant rivers and return it polluted? Can the City help to feed itself and provide a comfortable and healthy microclimate? The GCI, along with its partners, aims to move from merely dreaming about the existence of ideal African cities to making them a reality.

ACTIVISTS, SCIENTISTS AND A LIFETIME OF SERVICE:
PATRICK SOON-SHIONG AND MICHELE B. CHAN

From the Wits Medical School to Health Innovation

Dr Patrick Soon-Shiong and Michele B. Chan have it all: a partnership that has survived the inevitable challenges of life, a tight-knit family – they have two children – and a business empire that straddles media, medicine, telecommunications and energy. They are also the owners of a famous newspaper, part-owners of the Los Angeles Lakers basketball team, and proud Witsies.

Dr Patrick Soon-Shiong, founder and CEO of NantWorks and leader of the Cancer Moonshot 2020, at the Hyatt Regency Boston on 26 October 2016 in Boston, Massachusetts. Photo: Darren McCollester/Getty Images for NantHealth, Inc.

'How will I find God's particle in every human being every day as a way to treat patients? That connection is not obvious to many, but it's obvious to me.' Dr Patrick Soon-Shiong

The pair met on the Wits campus basketball courts, and it was at Wits that their formative years were spent and their values seeded. After leaving South Africa, they first relocated to Canada and then emigrated to the United States. Today, the two Hakka Chinese call Los Angeles (LA) their home.

Even before settling down and building their careers, both had already broken through significant South African ceilings. Chan was the first Chinese-South African student admitted into the Wits drama programme, and Soon-Shiong the first Chinese-South African doctor to intern at an apartheid-era hospital.

'The Asian way is to quietly pursue and do things without much fanfare,' Soon-Shiong notes. 'You are born inside the cauldron of inequality. You soon learn that to do well you have to be better.'

WITS REMEMBERED

Chan, who came from a sheltered background – her family didn't own a television and she attended an all-girls Catholic school – remembers her time at Wits in the mid-1970s as both exciting and challenging. One of the challenges was not knowing what was required in an audition, but the 17-year-old persevered nevertheless. Her tenacity paid off and she was selected as one of the 30 per cent of the 'people of colour' who applied and who were accepted into the drama programme. 'Acting was an incredible background for me,' says Chan, 'and Wits was an important start. As freshmen [undergraduates], we built The Nunnery – and physically painted it – because we didn't have a space to practise and perform. We used one of the classrooms as a make-up room. It was a magical time.'

But it was also an unbelievably difficult time. Chan was featured on an SABC television programme – only to be told that her shots had been cut because she was not white. The 1976 youth protests added to the confusion and fear and threw the spotlight on her identity.

Her time at Wits went on to serve her well. When the couple set up home in LA, Chan starred in a number of popular TV series, such as *MacGyver*, *Hotel* and *Danger Bay*, playing a variety of roles. Today she runs the media side of the NantWorks corporate empire – which has included revitalising the *Los Angeles Times* newspaper and commercialising new film technologies at the company's studios.

After graduating in the top five of his bachelor's of medicine (MBBCh) class at Wits, Soon-Shiong completed his internship at the Johannesburg General Hospital (today Charlotte Maxeke Johannesburg Academic Hospital). He returned to his hometown of East London, where he worked in a community clinic, treating children with tuberculosis. 'All I was doing was giving them an injection and food,' he recalls. 'I didn't know whether I was helping or hindering them. I decided that I needed to leave South Africa, learn about technology and come back. It was a promise I made to myself.'

'The biggest risk is not to follow your passion, and to live your life unfulfilled.' Dr Patrick Soon-Shiong

'The giants of Wits have all contributed to world medical knowledge – in HIV and heart and liver transplants, for example.'
Dr Patrick Soon-Shiong

After moving to Canada to complete his master's degree, he began surgical training at the University of California, Los Angeles (UCLA), becoming a board-certified surgeon and serving on the faculty as a surgeon and researcher. He shot to fame after he performed the first whole pancreas transplant and developed a diabetes treatment known as islet cell transplants. This treatment was patented and became Soon-Shiong's first major foray into private industry.

COMMERCIAL SUCCESS

Today, NantWorks is a billion-dollar multinational holding company with its headquarters in El Segundo, California. The company invests in everything from health technologies, energy, biosciences, communications and new media to telecoms. With a particular interest in sharing information, it is actively involved in semiconductors, artificial intelligence and supercomputing. Soon-Shiong remains involved at the founder level – he is CEO and chair – and one gets the impression that NantWorks has grown in different areas to reflect the couple's passions: for him, exploration and discovery feed his insatiable appetite for understanding the human condition, while Chan's exploration is through the lens of mixed media and the arts.

Soon-Shiong explains: 'I see the synapses in our brain as being no different from the packets of data going across the wireless lines. I see the need for generating energy so that we can power supercomputers. I see the need to understand carbon dioxide as how we breathe. This sounds crazy, disparate, but it's not – it's all interconnected. I see that very clearly in my head.'

Chan designed and built NantStudios, a state-of-the-art production facility that came into its own during the Covid-19 pandemic, with remote filming and production made possible through the technologies (especially data transmitting) created by the subsidiary companies. 'We complement each other,' Chan says with pride.

GIVING BACK

Together, the couple run two foundations, both dedicated to improving health, and they have pledged to give away at least half of their wealth to philanthropy through their commitment to the Giving Pledge.

Soon-Shiong has a keen sense of responsibility for the underdog. After hearing that a woman died due to being unable to get medical attention in a local hospital, he brought resources to improve the facility. 'This inner outrage has not stopped. Now we're in a privileged position to act with impact,' he says.

In a letter to the staff of the *LA Times* newspaper noting the #BlackLivesMatter movement and referencing their own experience with apartheid in a tone that was direct, empathetic and spoke to the dignity of all people, Chan stated: 'I've reached the stage in my career where this country has given me the opportunity. I've realised that we do have a choice to speak for the under-heard and to stand up for those who can't stand up for themselves.' She also sees the iconic newspaper as a means to grow local culture and to reposition Los Angeles as a media hub. 'I'm hoping to prove the *LA Times* to be a vibrant, self-sustaining voice of the West [United States] and to have a global impact – to shift the brand to be more inclusive and indicative of our society – we can do unique stories that have a global impact. I also hope to improve virtual production to bring Hollywood back to Hollywood – increase local production and make it more relevant.'

Their two children, one of whom works with community-based organisations in South Africa, have inherited this desire to help others in a meaningful way. 'In Chinese tradition, what we are doing is for the next generation,' says Chan. 'I tell my children, "Find your passion, be persistent, and pursue your dreams. Be patient, allow yourself to grow and flourish."'

THE PULL OF AFRICA
The couple are feeling the pull of Africa and plan to contribute to reducing inequality in medicine, building capacity in research and innovation, and collaborating with South African partners. To this end, Soon-Shiong has already made substantial funds available to be invested in vaccine manufacturing facilities, with South Africa as an entry point to the continent.

On a recent visit to support their daughter, who was working with South African non-profit organisations, they were impressed by what they saw. 'There's something in South Africa that is rare – a creative spirit or work ethic,' Soon-Shiong says. 'Many leading doctors in the world are South African and we see South Africa is positioned as a wonderful society, as a generation of young people who work together. My true passion is to build local capacity so that Africa can produce its own medicine – not just to bring in cheaper drugs from overseas. The giants of Wits have all contributed to world medical knowledge – in HIV and heart and liver transplants, for example.' He adds: 'Maybe now is the time to keep my inner promise.'

Soon-Shing participated in several webinars hosted by the dean of health sciences at Wits, Professor Shabir Madhi, a vaccinologist who seeks to develop South Africa's vaccine-producing capacity in order to benefit the continent. An A-rated scientist, Madhi led the AstraZeneca and Novavax Covid-19 vaccine trials in South Africa, and has made a major contribution to fighting the pandemic both in South Africa and beyond.

WE ARE GLOBAL

Leading the Charge

'I have not failed,' inventor Thomas Edison famously said. 'I've successfully found ten thousand ways that don't work.'

Indeed, in the medical research community, ineffective treatment trials often pave the way for new paths of enquiry. It was a series of such 'failures' that led Wits HIV scientists to prove that a two-monthly antiretroviral (ARV) injection is 89 per cent more effective than a daily pill in preventing HIV infections in women. The discovery made headlines worldwide in 2020 and is said to be a game-changer.

'Science is not only about success – it's also about learning from failure. After all, the first aircraft didn't fly,' says Professor Helen Rees, executive director of the Wits Reproductive Health and HIV Institute (Wits RHI), which led the research along with global partners. Rees and three other Wits women are at the forefront of the fight against HIV on the global stage and have been leading global scientists for decades. They share their incredible journeys.

A student from Wits University explains the HIV self-testing kit in Hillbrow, Johannesburg. Self-testing kits and vending machines distributing prescription drugs are two ways that HIV treatment is being automated to reduce stigma. Photo: Mujahid Safodien/AFP via Getty Images

EUREKA MOMENTS: PROFESSOR HELEN REES

After completing her medical training in the UK and serving as a paediatrician in Zimbabwe, Rees moved to South Africa in the early 1980s. While running paediatric services in Alexandra township, she developed the women's health policy for post-apartheid South Africa.

In 1994, Rees established the Wits RHI to support the new government in the development and implementation of sexual and reproductive health policies. The institute's early research focused on HIV prevention in women and adolescents.

Clinical research suggested that products such as female condoms, topical microbicides and daily antiretroviral tablets were effective but, in practice, the challenges women experienced in using them risked them being ineffective. 'The early microbicides required extraordinary discipline because they had to be placed in the vagina just before intercourse,' explains Rees. 'While daily antiretroviral tablets are highly effective in preventing HIV if used perfectly, women found it hard to take them regularly.'

These impediments set the Wits RHI on a search for imaginative technologies, culminating in the recent breakthrough ARV injection.

'Science is not only about success – it's also about learning from failure. After all, the first aircraft didn't fly.' Professor Helen Rees

It is one of many such advances. Rees was the principal investigator of the first South African HIV survey in adolescents that demonstrated high rates of HIV among young women, which had a profound impact on national and global programmes. As the lead researcher of the Evidence for Contraceptive Options and HIV Outcomes (ECHO) study, she answered the 30-year-old question about whether injectable contraception increases women's risk of acquiring HIV. The results disproved this concern.

Rees is recognised as a global expert on immunisation and vaccines. She established the African Leadership in Vaccinology Expertise consortium at Wits with Professor Shabir Madhi. As well as chairing the South African Health Products Regulatory Authority Board, Rees is a member of the Ministerial Advisory Committee (MAC) on Covid-19 vaccines and chairs the MAC Covid-19 Variant and Vaccines Technical Working Group. She is chair of the World Health Organization's African Regional Immunization Technical Advisory Group on Immunization and chairs the Global Alliance for Vaccines and Immunization Programme and Policy Committee. She is also a member of the board of the Coalition for Epidemic Preparedness and Innovation and chairs its Scientific Advisory Committee.

LEAPS AND BOUNDS: PROFESSOR GLENDA GRAY

Glenda Gray, research professor of paediatrics in the Wits School of Clinical Medicine, was a pioneer in the initial stages of the HIV pandemic. She is at the forefront of expanding HIV vaccine research in southern Africa. She is the co-principal investigator of the National Institutes of Health's HIV Vaccine Trials Network, which conducts over 80 per cent of candidate HIV vaccine clinical trials globally.

South African physician, scientist and activist specialising in the care of children and in HIV medicine, Wits research professor and alumna Glenda Gray. Photo: JP Crouch

'In the end, it's all about alleviating suffering.' Professor Glenda Gray

Gray fought fiercely for the distribution of ARVs, especially to prevent mother-to-child transmission, in the age of government AIDS denialism in the early 2000s. Today she is the president and CEO of the South African Medical Research Council. 'But I am and always will be a paediatrician first, and one who participates in health activism,' she says. This legacy started when she was completing her clinical training at the Chris Hani Baragwanath Academic Hospital in Soweto. 'I was a health activist determined to desegregate hospitals and became an HIV activist in the 1980s. Naturally, I turn to science to find solutions.'

Her first study showed that HIV-positive women in developing countries could safely feed their infants formula to avoid transmitting the virus through breastfeeding. At the time, health leaders argued that the risks of contaminated water in formula outweighed that of contracting HIV through breast milk. 'I didn't think that white men from the Northern Hemisphere should make decisions for Black African women,' she says wryly.

In 1996, together with Professor James McIntyre, Gray co-founded the Wits Perinatal HIV Research Unit (PHRU), a world-renowned entity focused on HIV prevention and treatment. Among its many successes, the PHRU demonstrated that the early use of ARVs in children could reduce mortality by two thirds – a revolutionary step in the treatment of HIV in children at a global level.

SPACE AND PLACE

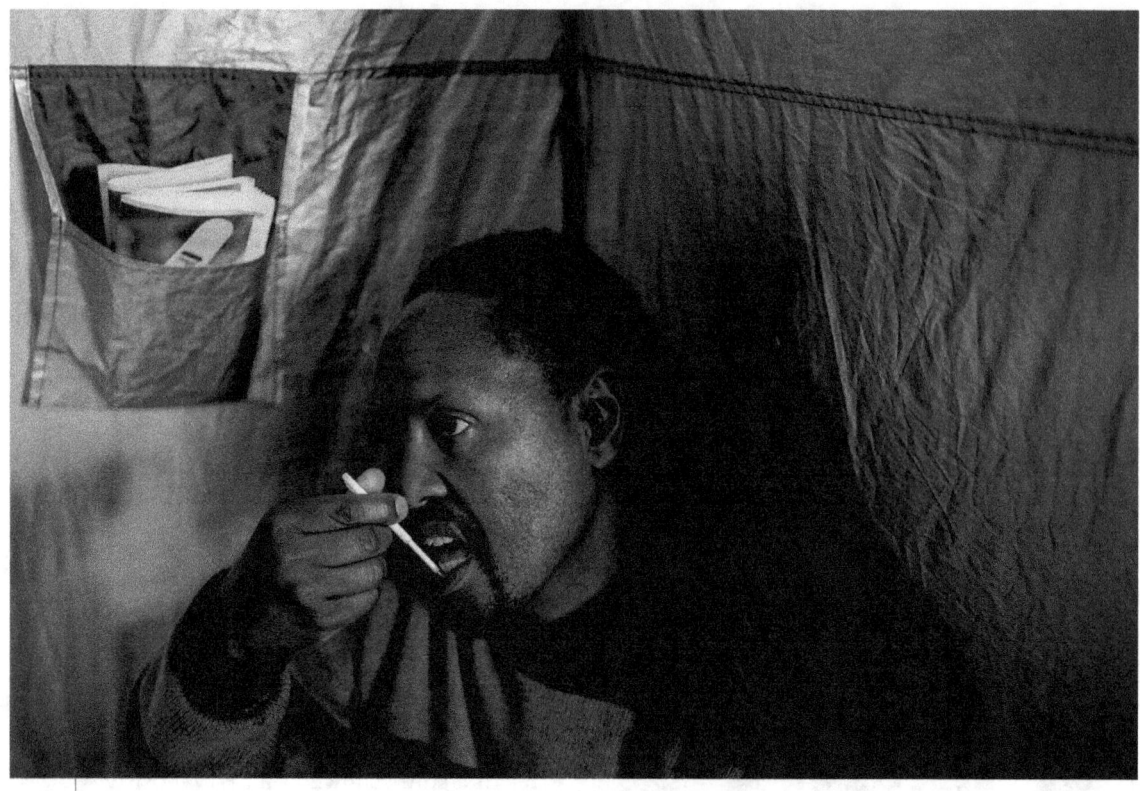

Forty-five-year-old Oscar Tyumre uses an HIV self-testing kit, administered by students from Wits University, on 19 March 2018. Photo: Mujahid Safodien/AFP via Getty Images

UNRAVELLING CLUES:
PROFESSOR CAROLINE TIEMESSEN
In 2017 and 2018, Professor Caroline Tiemessen, research professor in the School of Pathology, was making headlines for her involvement in two HIV-related cases.

The first was a child who had suppressed the virus for nine years and remains HIV-negative today. The child had received ARVs as an infant with high viral load counts, but treatment was stopped at 50 weeks. 'Our journey started when the child was nine years old and tested like an uninfected child. We applied more sensitive methods and did lots of additional work. To date, all we have found are fragments of HIV

'Awards are nice, but I get more excited by the science itself. I like a challenge. I'm not sure if everything is answerable, but I'd like to try.' Professor Caroline Tiemessen

DNA. We believe that these fragments aren't able to infect new cells,' says Tiemesssen.

This, of course, leaves many more questions, and uncovering the answers could take time, Tiemessen acknowledges. 'I feel an enormous responsibility to choose the most informative tests, and to find clues that can help eliminate HIV in children,' she says.

The second case that made headlines was the first living donor partial liver transplant from an HIV-positive mother to her HIV-negative child. Even though it could have meant virus transmission, the child would have died without the transplant. Both mother and child were given ARVs and the team still cannot detect the virus in the child, even with very sensitive tests.

Professor Tiemessen is head of the Cell Biology Research Laboratory in the Centre for HIV and Sexually Transmitted Infections at the National Institute for Communicable Diseases, as well as a Department of Science and Innovation–National Research Foundation (DSI-NRF) chair of HIV Vaccine Translational Research. She has received a plethora of awards for this and other work. 'Awards are nice, but I get more excited by the science itself. I like a challenge. I'm not sure if everything is answerable, but I'd like to try.'

LEADING FROM THE FRONT: PROFESSOR LYNN MORRIS

Professor Lynn Morris was appointed as the deputy vice-chancellor: research and innovation at Wits University in 2021. Aside from her extensive leadership experience in the healthcare sector, the A-rated scientist is renowned globally for her scientific work in understanding the antibody response to HIV and is responsible for conducting validated end-point assays for HIV vaccine clinical trials.

The former executive director of the National Institute for Communicable Diseases, Morris led the institute through two major health crises: the listeria outbreak of 2017/18 and the Covid-19 pandemic. 'The success of the Covid-19 vaccine will rely on the majority of people agreeing to be vaccinated as quickly as possible – an effort that is being undermined by those who use fake science and misinformation to cast doubt on vaccines,' says Morris. 'But most importantly, what the Covid-19 pandemic has demonstrated is that if there is political will and a co-ordinated and well-funded global effort, vaccine development can proceed exceedingly fast. There is no doubt that new pathogenic viruses will continue to emerge. Let's build on what we have learned from the Covid-19 pandemic so we can respond more rapidly and effectively to viral threats, including HIV, which still remains one of the world's biggest health challenges.'

Morris won the Wits Vice-Chancellor's Research Award in 2014, the South African Medical Research Council's Gold Medal in 2015, the prestigious Harry Oppenheimer Fellowship Award in 2017 and the World Academy of Sciences Prize in Medical Sciences in 2018.

SPACE AND PLACE

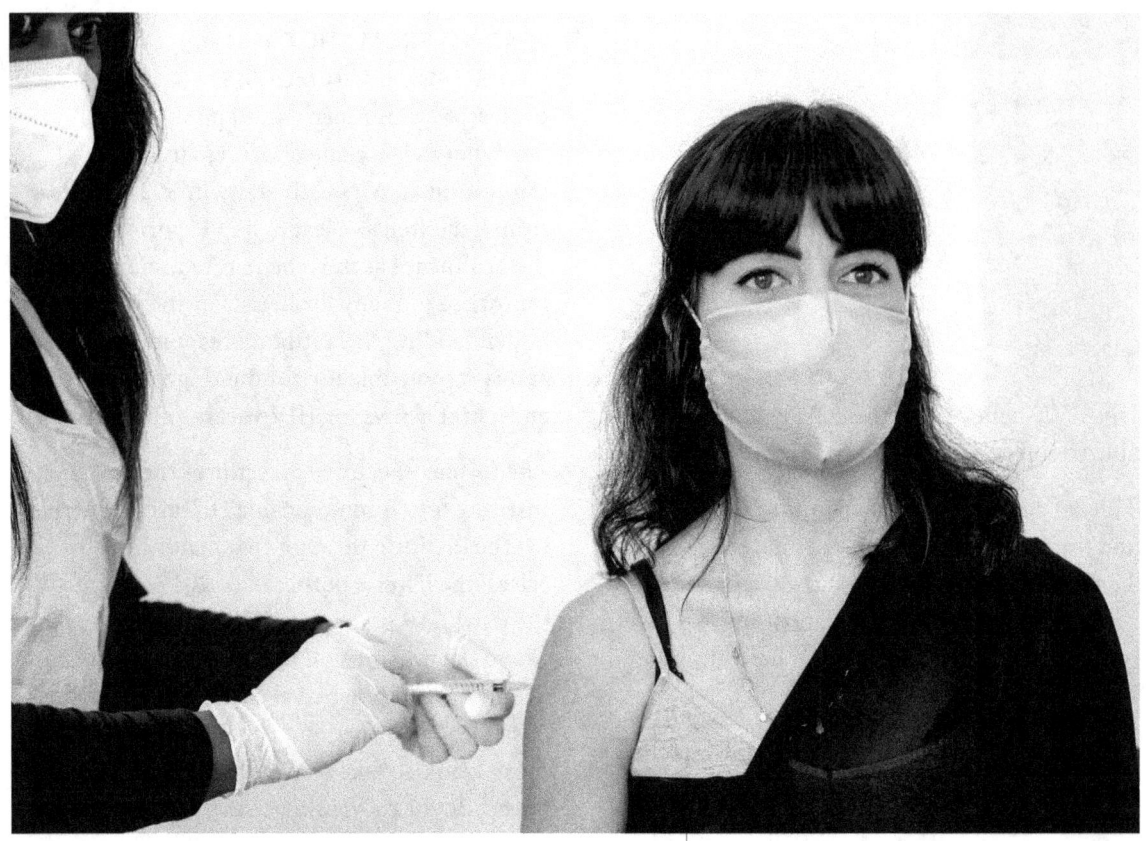

Robyn Porteous, a vaccine trials volunteer, is injected with a vaccine as part of the country's human clinical trial for potential vaccines after being tested for the coronavirus disease (Covid-19), at the Wits RHI Shandukani Research Centre in Johannesburg, 27 August 2020. Photo: Siphiwe Sibeko/REUTERS

THE OTHER PANDEMIC: COVID-19

If anyone can find answers, it is these four women. While their HIV work never sleeps, Professors Rees, Gray, Tiemessen and Morris all applied their expertise to aid the fight against Covid-19 when the worldwide pandemic took hold.

Tiemessen studied hospitalised Covid-19 patients to find immune and genetic traits that could predict how a patient would fare in fighting off the disease. Rees serves on the World Health Organization's Covid-19 Emergency Committee and chairs the Scientific Advisory Committee for the Coalition for Epidemic Preparedness and Innovation. Her work as chair of the Global Alliance for Vaccines and Immunisation Programme and Policy Committee is in part to ensure equitable vaccine distribution, which will be essential for South Africa in the long term. She also secured tranches of vaccines for South Africans as part of the trial which she led in South Africa.

'The success of the Covid-19 vaccine will rely on the majority of people agreeing to be vaccinated as quickly as possible – an effort that is being undermined by those who use fake science and misinformation to cast doubt on vaccines.' Professor Lynn Morris

Gray served as chair of the Covid-19 Research Sub-Committee with 50 expert Covid-19 advisers. 'One of the best things about my work is that it allows me to position science to be responsive to real life,' she says. 'Throughout my career, I've always been proudest of those moments. Research and policy mean little if not put into practice. In the end, it's all about alleviating suffering.'[15] Gray also served as the co-principal investigator in the Sisonke Covid-19 vaccine study to protect healthcare workers.[16]

Bhekokuzakuye 'Keith' Mdlalose with the Johannesburg skyline in the background, photographed on the rooftop of a Wits building. Photo: Daniel Born

ACTIVISTS, SCIENTISTS AND A LIFETIME OF SERVICE:
BHEKOKUZAKUYE 'KEITH' MDLALOSE

An Honest Man

The frail but erect frame of a man walking with pride gives no clues that he holds an important position in Protection Services at Wits University. Only when his face is digitally scanned so that he can enter the central command offices does it reveal the respect he inspires from the other officers.

'Be honest in everything that you do.'
Bhekokuzakuye Mdlalose

Bhekokuzakuye Mdlalose – also known as 'Keith' – is a long-serving employee at Wits and a wholly self-made man. He lives by one mantra: 'Be honest in everything that you do.'

Mdlalose moved to Johannesburg in 1985 because his father worked at the then Baragwanath Hospital. With a matric certificate but no knowledge of the security sector, he nevertheless successfully applied for a security position at Wits. It wasn't long before he realised that he had found his passion. He enrolled in a few evening classes in order to improve his chances of career progression, with his first goal being to reach supervisor level.

Robert Kemp, a supervisor in the Campus Control unit as it was known, mentored Mdlalose. 'He taught me two things,' Mdlalose recalls. 'To be honest and to work hard. He would say to me, "When the truth comes out, you will be embarrassed." He told me to tell the truth no matter what, even if it is a security colleague who had stolen something. I was short-tempered, but he taught me to be calm at all times. As a unionist, I knew how to argue. I had to teach myself to stay calm no matter what happens.'

Mdlalose, a father of three, sees himself as a lifelong learner. He learned computer skills and became a supervisor after joining the Wits investigations section in 1996, a post that he held for 20 years. He has held the position of security manager since 2016.

RISE OF TECHNOLOGY

In 35 years on the job, Mdlalose has seen the rise of technology and how it has improved the University's security systems. He laughs as he recalls the 1980s: 'We had only one typist for the whole department – we had to queue to get our cases typed up and it could sometimes take up to a week to get the completed documents returned to us.'

The University had no perimeter walls, resulting in numerous break-ins into motor vehicles and buildings. Wits had no cameras on the campus, only seven alarms and 60 security staff. Today the University has enhanced its digital and personnel security measures to better protect Wits students, staff and property.

STUCK IN THE MIDDLE

A career spanning a fair amount of tumultuous South African political history has seen Mdlalose stuck more than once between different parties with competing interests, and he admits to having had to face some challenging moments. In the 1980s, during anti-apartheid protests, Mdlalose and his team had to ensure that no harm came to the University students and staff from the South African Police Services. During the #FeesMustFall protests, he says, 'the students wanted to enter the Great Hall and management told me this was not allowed. I told the students that this could not happen, but they entered anyway.'

One of the outcomes of the #FeesMustFall movement proved to be a challenge for Mdlalose when Protection Services had to insource all the campus contract security officers (by far the majority of officers), train them to comply with

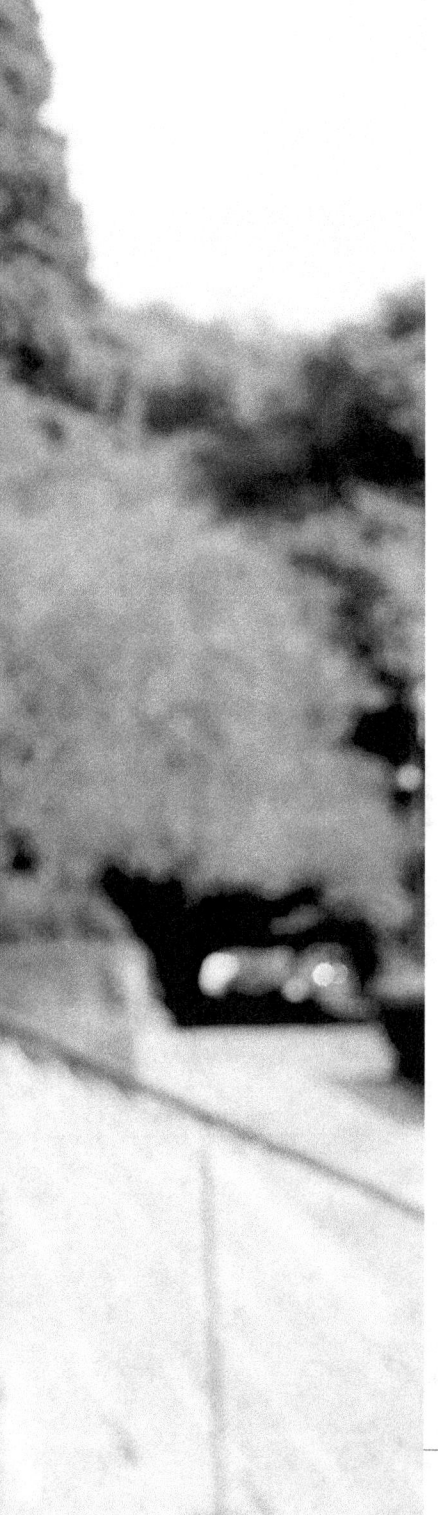

'People can achieve anything they want – through hard work.'
Bhekokuzakuye Mdlalose

Wits standards, and integrate them into the culture of the department. While it was quite a task, it further improved the University's ability to protect students, staff, visitors and its property.

TOMORROW STARTS HERE
Mdlalose is nearing the end of his time at Wits. When he retires, he says that he plans to move to his cattle farm in KwaZulu-Natal, near Greytown. His children are all professionals or studying, and he is looking forward to spending more time with his wife – he drives home to see her every month. He is proud of the important role that he has played at Wits and remains steadfast in his passion for the job: 'I always say to new employees, "Tomorrow starts here at Wits! No one is after you if you do your job. You must tell yourself that you are doing it for your own benefit – whatever you are doing." People can achieve anything they want – through hard work.'

Security manager at Wits University, Bhekokuzakuye 'Keith' Mdlalose has been on the job for over 35 years. Photo: Daniel Born

The new walk-in entrance on Jan Smuts Avenue provides a safe, well-lit entrance to East Campus for students who enter the university on foot.

Photo: Shivan Parusnath

Photo: Daniel Born

03

The Future

OVERVIEW

The place of the university in society has changed radically in the last century, not least of all in South Africa. The university was an institution originally designed to play essentially an elitist role in society – accepting only a tiny proportion of the population into a highly specialised life of learning and training in select disciplines.

Now, the university has transformed into a more democratic institution, and for young people it is seen to be one of the best ways to counter poverty and unemployment, particularly in an unequal country like South Africa. As such, universities around the world, including Wits, have prioritised access to quality higher education.

Wits grew from 19 000 students in 1999 to about 40 000 students in 2021. Digital transformation is one of the key components of the University's strategic plan for 2023 to 2033, and while Wits will remain a contact teaching and learning university, it seeks to create greater access to learning opportunities through its digital online offerings. Smart classrooms, future libraries, knowledge hubs, simulation laboratories, innovation precincts, e-zones and blended learning options are all in play. Wits' new digital suite includes full online programmes and e-degrees, short courses and many free Massive Open Online Courses (MOOCs) that have registered over 100 000 learners from around the globe. In addition, the high-tech eFundanathi (Learn with Us) eZone is a student-centred adaptive learning environment that uses cutting-edge technology and advanced eLearning tools to deliver education that prepares students for the twenty-first century.

Wits is acutely aware of its responsibility to enable social and economic progress across Africa, and to deliver on its social impact and research mandate to address the challenges of the twenty-first century, from its locale in the Global South. The University has embraced digital transformation and health innovation in its research, teaching and innovation spheres. It is the first university in Africa to host a 5G lab, and the first university to access quantum computing on the continent through its partnership with IBM. Wits offers advanced programmes in artificial intelligence, big data, software engineering and the digital arts, amongst others. Researchers have used high-resolution scanning and 3D printing to

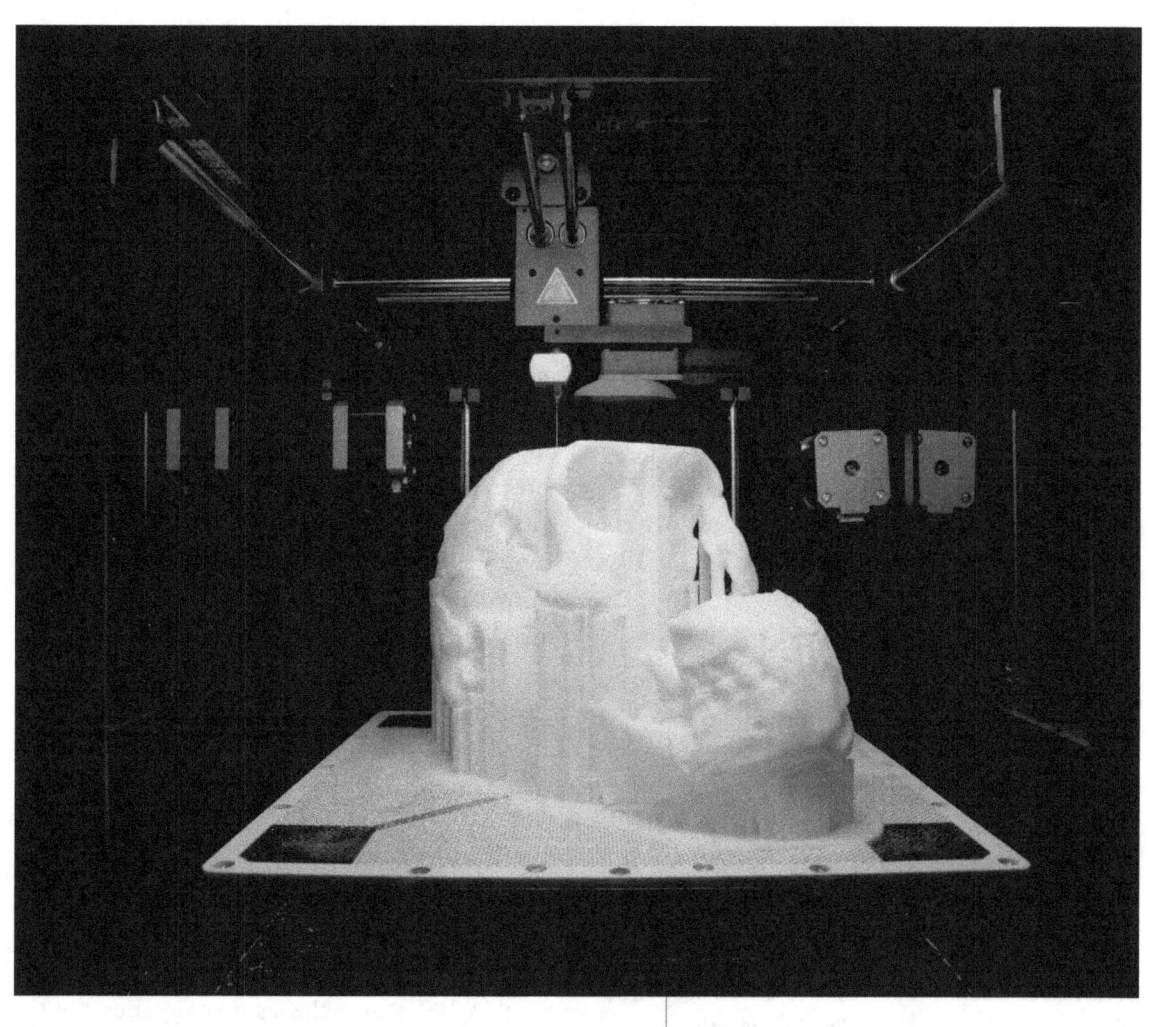

A 3D-printed skull of a new human ancestor, Homo naledi, is seen shortly after being printed at Wits. Photo: Daniel Born

reproduce casts of fossils embedded in rock, and students used 3D printing to produce custom-made face shields for healthcare workers in hospitals during the coronavirus pandemic.

The response to the Covid-19 pandemic provided an insight into the future of the University through the introduction of remote and emergency learning and teaching, transitioning to full online teaching and learning, and the navigation of new powerful, cloud-based learning management systems. In 2020, Wits took the academic project (about 3 000 programmes) online in three weeks, no easy feat for a traditionally contact university. Laptops and mobile learning devices were couriered to students across the country, data was provided, and negotiations with mobile telephone operators ensured that the majority of educational sites could be easily accessed at no cost to students.

INFLUENTIAL COLLABORATIVE NETWORKS

Wits has developed strategic local and international collaborative networks in academia and with the public and private sectors and civil society. The University is fully engaged with the contemporary, interconnected world, and works across disciplines, faculties and institutions to find solutions to real-world challenges.

Wits is also home to several specialised academic and research units, which develop creative solutions to real-world problems. For example, Professor Bavesh Kana, of the Department of Science and Innovation–National Research Foundation Centre of Excellence for Biomedical TB Research, and Professor Lesley Scott, of the Research Diagnostics Laboratory, developed technology using molecular diagnostics that ensures the efficacy of the equipment that tests for tuberculosis. The technology increased access to TB testing, which improved the diagnosis and treatment of TB around the world, and ultimately inhibited further infection. They then developed the SmartSpot technology which guarantees the quality of the molecular diagnostic tests, and which is used in more than 30 countries worldwide.

Another innovation, from the School of Electrical and Information Engineering, has reached commercialisation stage and will undoubtedly impact on the lives of people living in rural and unserviced communities. The Personal Consumer Grid innovation is a home-based electrical off-grid solution that easily integrates renewable energy sources along with batteries and appliances, for the electrification of households in Africa. This expandable solution ensures that as a household can afford more solar panels or wind generators, batteries or 12V appliances, these components are easily added to the system, with no need for a trained person to install them.

THE WITS INSTITUTE FOR SOCIAL AND ECONOMIC RESEARCH

The Wits Institute for Social and Economic Research (WiSER) was first established by prominent sociologist Professor Deborah Posel in 2001. Over the last two decades, the institute's interdisciplinary research in the humanities and social sciences has become a benchmark in Africa, and increasingly globally. The institute emphasises the importance of the Global South as an area of research focus and as a means of focusing interdisciplinary research away from the previously dominant paradigm of Western Europe and the US in academic disciplines. It draws on a history of advanced interdisciplinary research at Wits that dates back to the late 1960s, but over the last ten years it has pursued critical enquiry into the complexities and paradoxes of change in South Africa, drawing on comparative international research from leading scholars, especially from Africa. It has also provided an institutional space that strengthens the scholarly dialogue between South African researchers and academics in the rest of the world.

THE CENTRE FOR RESEARCHING EDUCATION AND LABOUR

The Centre for Researching Education and Labour (REAL), founded in 1987 as the Wits Education Policy Unit (EPU), was at the time one of only four university-based research units in the education space. The EPU was to provide a scholarly context for the development of post-apartheid education policy. It provided policy support, research and analysis to the democratic movement and national and provincial governments. Aligned to the changing context and new educational demands in a democratic South Africa, the REAL Centre, based in the Wits School of Education, was established in 2012 to deepen the understanding of the complex relationships between education, knowledge, work, the economy and society. As such, it explores these relationships to promote social, economic and ecological sustainability and a more just society. The centre continues to undertake transformational collaborative educational work with the public sector and government.

THE AFRICAN CENTRE FOR MIGRATION AND SOCIETY

The African Centre for Migration and Society has become Africa's leading scholarly institution for research and teaching on human mobility. Established in 1993, the ACMS is an independent, interdisciplinary and internationally engaged institution that seeks to understand the relationships between human movement, politics, poverty and social transformation, and conducts research collaboratively across sub-Saharan Africa, with partnerships in Asia, Europe and the Americas. Diaspora, refugee and migrant populations are a crucial dimension of the modern political and social experience, and the centre partners with organisations in government and civil society to identify data needs, conduct research and shape policy.

THE GAUTENG CITY-REGION OBSERVATORY

Providing appropriate and effective knowledge frameworks for the growth of cities within the province, the Gauteng City-Region Observatory (GCRO) is a partnership between Wits, the University of Johannesburg and the Gauteng provincial government which seeks to share and create knowledge through interaction with academia, knowledge councils, private sector think-tanks, non-governmental research organisations, and information-exchange and learning networks.

The GCRO provides planning and management resources for the fast-growing and dynamic urban region that is Gauteng, one of a few city-regions around the world. This spans the provincial boundaries of Gauteng into the economic and transport corridors to the east and west, and incorporates planning around all the major urban centres in Gauteng. Better planning, management and co-operative governance relies on improved communication, data analysis and reflective evaluation. The GCRO is charged with building strategic intelligence for the city-region and conducts research on population movement, transport infrastructure, economic data, job profiles and employment data in order to optimise the development of the city-region.

THE SOUTHERN CENTRE FOR INEQUALITY STUDIES

The Southern Centre for Inequality Studies has embarked on a multi-partner research and policy project focusing on understanding and addressing inequality in the Global South. While technical solutions to address inequality are very important, they will not be politically feasible unless the social and political forces driving high levels of inequality are clearly understood and have been addressed. Inequality is a global problem, and studying and addressing it in South Africa will enable meaningful dialogues about inequality in other settings across the Global South.

The centre identifies key areas where inequality shapes the life chances of individuals and aims, through a focus on the structure of the economy and society as well as political, economic and cultural processes, to understand the production, reproduction and intersection of power relations and inequality. It also seeks to reimagine alternative configurations of power relations that would generate affirmative state action, provide greater equality of access to relevant resources, and fundamentally alter the structure of power relations in society. Developing a research and policy agenda for the inclusive growth of productive forces is also on the cards.

THE WITS CENTRE FOR DIVERSITY STUDIES

The aim of this centre is to build capacity to meet the challenges of diverse societies, especially in post-apartheid South Africa, through interdisciplinary postgraduate education and research. Grounded in social justice imperatives, the centre has adapted a racial literacy concept to analyse other axes of oppression, such as gender, sexuality, disability and class amongst others, in order to describe the field of critical diversity studies. The critical diversity studies lens opens up challenging research questions which emerge at the interstices of current disciplinary boundaries. These questions have the capacity to shift common-sense assumptions about the social, enabling fresh and penetrating analyses of current social challenges.

DIGITAL TRANSFORMATION

Wits is at the forefront of driving the development of cutting-edge digital technologies for the twenty-first century – from artificial intelligence and machine learning, to big data, blockchain and the Internet of Things. Wits is also helping organisations and businesses to go digital and is pioneering the adoption of innovative digital technology in many sectors, including mining, education, finance, art, medicine and journalism, amongst others.

The Gauteng City-Region Observatory (GCRO) provides planning and management resources for the fast-growing and dynamic urban region that is Gauteng. Some of the GCRO's award-winning research explores the potential for infrastructure transitions to meet the growing demand for urban-based amenities, while building a more just and sustainable city-region. Photo: Andiswa Mkosi for the GCRO

TSHIMOLOGONG

Wits University's Tshimologong Digital Innovation Precinct, in Braamfontein, was established in 2016.

The precinct provides a space for innovation to take place across disciplines and sectors, and combines it with entrepreneurship that results in the gestation of new ideas, projects, ventures and viable businesses. A recent example is the joint venture between Wits, Huawei and service provider rain to launch Africa's first 5G laboratory.

The collaboration provides students with access to a live 5G environment and applications, knowledge of the technology's applications for the local market, smart/safe campus initiatives, and augmented and virtual reality applications.

Short for 'fifth-generation wireless technology', 5G provides digital cellular networks with faster upload and download speeds, numerous Internet applications, enterprise networking, and critical communications services. The 5G Innovation Lab is a first for South Africa and the continent.

THE ROBOTICS, AUTONOMOUS INTELLIGENCE AND LEARNING LAB

The Robotics, Autonomous Intelligence and Learning Lab at Wits is an innovative, future-focused research group concentrating on artificial intelligence, machine learning and robotics. The lab contributes to research in the fields of computer vision and the theory of deep networks, and applies its findings to diverse areas in the public and private sectors, such as healthcare and education.

SCILINX

Scilinx Research is a business solution design and research laboratory based in the School of Computer Science and Applied Mathematics. The laboratory assists businesses to improve their operational capabilities in different sectors of the economy by using machine learning, applied maths, human behavioural sciences and organisational theory. These fields offer innovative insights in areas such as strategy operationalisation, operational processes design and technology design. The laboratory also offers business applications that range from the optimisation of factory production line design to providing a competitive advantage in an enterprise risk-management scenario.

OVERVIEW

Mpho Makutu creates robots at the MakerSpace in the Tshimologong Digital Innovation Precinct in Braamfontein. Photo: Daniel Born

The exterior of the IBM centre at the Tshimologong Precinct in Braamfontein. Photo: Daniel Born

THE FUTURE

THE JOBURG CENTRE FOR SOFTWARE ENGINEERING

At the vanguard of the University's programme of innovative interaction with the private sector and with developments in the digital economy is the Joburg Centre for Software Engineering (JCSE), established in 2005 as a partnership between government, industry and the University. The centre was initially focused on developing and growing the software development sector of the local ICT industry. Programmes were created to develop skills, to promote the adoption of international best practices and to encourage transformation in the sector. The JCSE has a strong focus on research and innovation, and has conducted numerous research projects, including an annual ICT Skills Survey and contract research for both government and industry.

FAK'UGESI

Proving that technology collaboration is not reserved for industry and commerce, Wits has been the starting point for a unique 'creative technology' initiative. Fak'ugesi, which means 'switch it on' or 'add power' in urban Zulu, was the name chosen for the annual Fak'ugesi African Digital Innovation Festival. The focus of the festival is on culture, technology and innovation in Africa. It is a truly interdisciplinary showcase of technology, digital arts and culture, including gaming, sound, interactive virtual reality and artificial intelligence applications. It was founded in 2014 as a collaboration between the Tshimologong Digital Innovation Precinct and the Wits Digital Arts Department. Its collaborative ethos has seen the festival work with the School of Electrical and Information Engineering, Wits Music and many external contributors. An

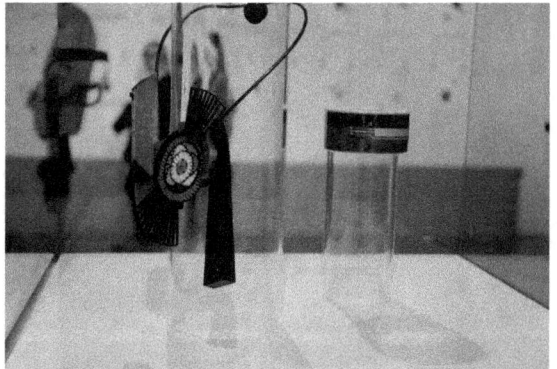

Wits engineering student Xolani Radebe developed a drone with a built-in thermal camera that can detect the body temperature of large groups of people in vast areas such as in malls, on campuses or in other busy places. Photo: Shivan Parusnath

The Digital Imaginaries: Premonition exhibition, tied to the Fak'ugesi African Digital Innovation Festival, for which Wits School of Arts lecturer Dr Tegan Bristow is principal researcher. Artist Ling Tan's wearable device detects safety levels in Braamfontein. Source: Wits Art Museum

underlying belief for Fak'ugesi Festival organisers is that a strong connection must be made to African cultural practices and creative encounters for innovation technology to succeed.

ENSURING BETTER HEALTH FOR ALL
Wits is home to one of the best health sciences faculties on the continent and graduates more specialists than any other university in Africa. Students train in some of the largest hospitals in the Southern Hemisphere and work on the front line with talented, caring healthcare professionals. Wits' reach extends to care and treatment in clinics throughout the country, including at the Wits Rural Facility in Mpumalanga, which serves as a hub for interdisciplinary and longitudinal research.

DID YOU KNOW?

The Wits Donald Gordon Medical Centre – the first and only private teaching hospital in South Africa – provides highly specialised training across a range of critically required speciality and sub-speciality disciplines.

One of the world's largest and most impactful university-based health companies, the Wits Health Consortium – with an annual turnover greater than R2.5 billion generated through its extensive contract clinical research and related activities – places Wits as one of the world's leading universities in terms of the proportion of total income generated through commercialisation activities.

Wits attracts significant donor support for key community training, clinical and research facilities, including the R70 million Wits McAlpine Burns Unit at Chris Hani Baragwanath Academic Hospital opened in 2021, the new R22 million Advanced Surgical Skills Lab opened in 2021, the Zola Clinic in Soweto, and the Agincourt Research facility in Mpumalanga, which are all flagship centenary projects.

The Faculty of Health Sciences' 24 research entities publish more than 1 500 papers per year in leading high-impact international journals.

Wits graduates the highest number of medical specialists and sub-specialists in South Africa – 80 per cent of Wits medical students pass the Fellowship of the College of Physicians clinical examinations, compared to the national average pass rate of 50 per cent.

Professor Shabir Madhi has been leading Covid-19 vaccine trials in South Africa. Photo: Shivan Parusnath

The Wits Faculty of Health Sciences has over 1 000 research collaborations with global universities and research institutions on all continents. Its strength lies in its excellent education and training, and its many globally recognised research entities. Wits understands the interconnections between infectious and communicable diseases, bioinformatics and molecular biosciences, the future of precision medicine and genetics, public healthcare systems and management, and the ethical and governance issues implicit in these fields. This places Wits in good stead to lead health innovation in the country.

The faculty has played a critical role in responding to the effects of the Covid-19 pandemic on multiple levels. Researchers, scientists, academics and clinicians have been at the forefront of helping to predict, understand

Medical students at the Wits Parktown Health Sciences campus. Photo: Shivan Parusnath

and contain Covid-19; manage the public health and socio-economic impact on society; and develop prevention, care and treatment regimens based on sound research.

Professor Shabir Madhi, executive director of the South African Medical Research Council Vaccines and Infectious Diseases Analytics Research Unit and dean of the Faculty of Health Sciences, has led two Covid-19 vaccine trials – the 'Oxford trial', in association with Oxford University, the Jenner Institute and AstraZeneca, and the 'Novavax trial' with US-based biotechnology firm Novavax – both global trials.[17]

A Covid-19 website portal provides the Wits community with regular updates, the latest research and teaching news, educational and advocacy campaigns and policy updates.[18]

NETWORKS THAT IMPACT THE WORLD

Wits has established important formal collaborative relationships with many universities around the world. The University co-founded the African Research Universities Alliance (ARUA), which was launched in March 2015, bringing together 16 research-intensive universities on the continent. The alliance seeks to enhance the quality of research conducted in Africa by African researchers and brings together several peer institutions that work together to support researchers in different fields.

Wits is also a member of the Association of Commonwealth Universities, which promotes and represents the university sector at governmental level across the Commonwealth. The University has become a member of the prestigious Association of African Universities, established in Ghana in 1963 to promote and facilitate networking, collaboration and shared experiences in teaching, learning and research and to provide effective representation of the African higher education community in regional and international affairs. In 2021, Wits renewed its memorandum of understanding with the University of Edinburgh to collaborate on academic, research and innovation projects.

Many Wits scientists and students conduct world-class science research at the SA-European Council for Nuclear Research (CERN) in Geneva, at the European Synchroton Radiation Facility (ESRF) in France and at many other world-class facilities across the globe.

WE LEAD CHANGE

Light Years Ahead: Invention, Innovation and the Structured Light Lab

Researchers at the Structured Light Laboratory at Wits are currently exploring a revolutionary concept using light beams to convey data and communication through light. It all started in 2015 in an empty room in the School of Physics, where researchers aimed to explore ways of tailoring light beams to make a practical impact.

Postdoctoral student Wagner Tavares Buono (left) and student Keshaan Singh (right) are aligning their laser beams through lenses so that they can shape the polarisation and spatial pattern of laser beams using digital micro-mirror devices. Photo: Daniel Born

Lured from private industry to Wits through the Distinguished Professors programme, Professor Andrew Forbes became the leader of the laboratory. His strong leaning towards novel technologies was a major attraction for students drawn to innovation, and with the support of external funders and industry, Forbes and his team published over 100 papers in five years, many in prestigious journals and several making international news.

The team has spent many years developing ways of communicating via light quickly and securely. 'The challenge is, how do we create, detect and transfer patterns of light through space?' asks Professor Forbes. 'Present technology makes use of only one pattern of light. What if we could use ten patterns of light, each pattern carrying data? The result would be ten times the present bandwidth.'

THE FUTURE

Forbes explains that they are developing methods of tailoring light, much like cloth is tailored, for applications in various fields – not just fast and secure communication to bridge the digital divide, but also for other uses that relate to imaging, health and metrology. One interesting example is how light can be used to measure the facial features of truck drivers at night to make sure that they are alert; another is how light can be used to safely probe environmental pollutants.

CREATING NEW KNOWLEDGE

In many projects, the team has taken existing optical communication technology and made that technology better, sometimes incrementally through engineering solutions, and sometimes through radical approaches based on new physics, thereby generating new knowledge.

Forbes indicates that the team will launch a new communications solution that addresses real-life challenges. This innovation will change the way people communicate in areas where there is no Wi-Fi, fibre or cellular connectivity. Rescuers, for example, will be able to stay in contact with each other in disaster areas while they search for survivors and victims of earthquakes, floods or fires, in places where roads and other infrastructure have been damaged and phone lines and fibre cables destroyed. It will also be an advantage for people working in environmentally sensitive areas as they will not need to inflict any damage on the environment by setting up traditional means of communication.

The laboratory has deliberately chosen specific applications. 'What you can do in the lab is determined by the calibre of the team, and at Wits we have excellent talent to tackle complex problems,' says Forbes. 'I'm very careful about choosing the type of projects that we can tackle, and we try to determine beforehand the problems that are likely to emerge. We are achieving [at] what would be considered [a] very fast [rate] in the academic world. It's all about invention and innovation – coming up with ideas and turning those ideas into functional technology.'

The team collaborates closely with existing creators of fibre optics. 'We don't think South Africa should be the net importers of technology,' says Forbes. 'We are motivated to solve problems. We argue that we live in the century of the photon [photonics], with light-based technologies replacing electronics, and we want to be ahead of the game. We aim for economic impact so that our innovations have practical, profitable applications.'

A student aligning a quantum set-up for generating quantum-entangled photo pairs. Photo: Daniel Born

The Structured Light Laboratory team at Wits has won over 100 awards for outstanding contributions to science, including major national and international prizes.

THE FUTURE

Postdoctoral student Valeria Rodriguez-Fajardo guides a laser beam to a spatial light modulator so that it can be imprinted with spatial patterns. Photo: Daniel Born

IMPACT AROUND THE WORLD

The work undertaken by the laboratory is attracting international attention, especially in academic circles. Forbes has received applications from a number of excellent postdoctoral students from as far afield as Iran, Colombia and Brazil. They all want to work at the Structured Light Laboratory because it is involved in conducting science at the highest level. 'Once they've been involved in the projects we do here, they go back home with an excellent set of skills,' says Forbes. He and his students have won over 100 awards for outstanding contributions to science, including major national and international prizes.

'It would be wonderful if we can get more international postdoctoral students. We are considered one of the best in the world at what we do,' says Forbes. 'I don't believe that we should

'Be creative, take risks, dream big and think differently from everyone else. This is the path to advancement and success.' Professor Andrew Forbes

train photonics students for academic positions. I'm very passionate about seeing the photonic and quantum industries grow in South Africa. I'd like to see our students make a living by developing or joining commercial companies in these industries. There are many opportunities in the mainstream where applying science and knowledge can benefit the technology sector, and society more broadly. Through the Structured Light Laboratory, Wits has an outlet for new ideas, and taking those ideas into the mainstream will create a very good ecosystem.'

Forbes has some final advice for his students and prospective researchers who want to be part of the Structured Light Lab team: 'Be creative, take risks, dream big and think differently from everyone else. This is the path to advancement and success.'

Professor Andrew Forbes (centre) and some of his Structured Light Laboratory students. Photo: Daniel Born

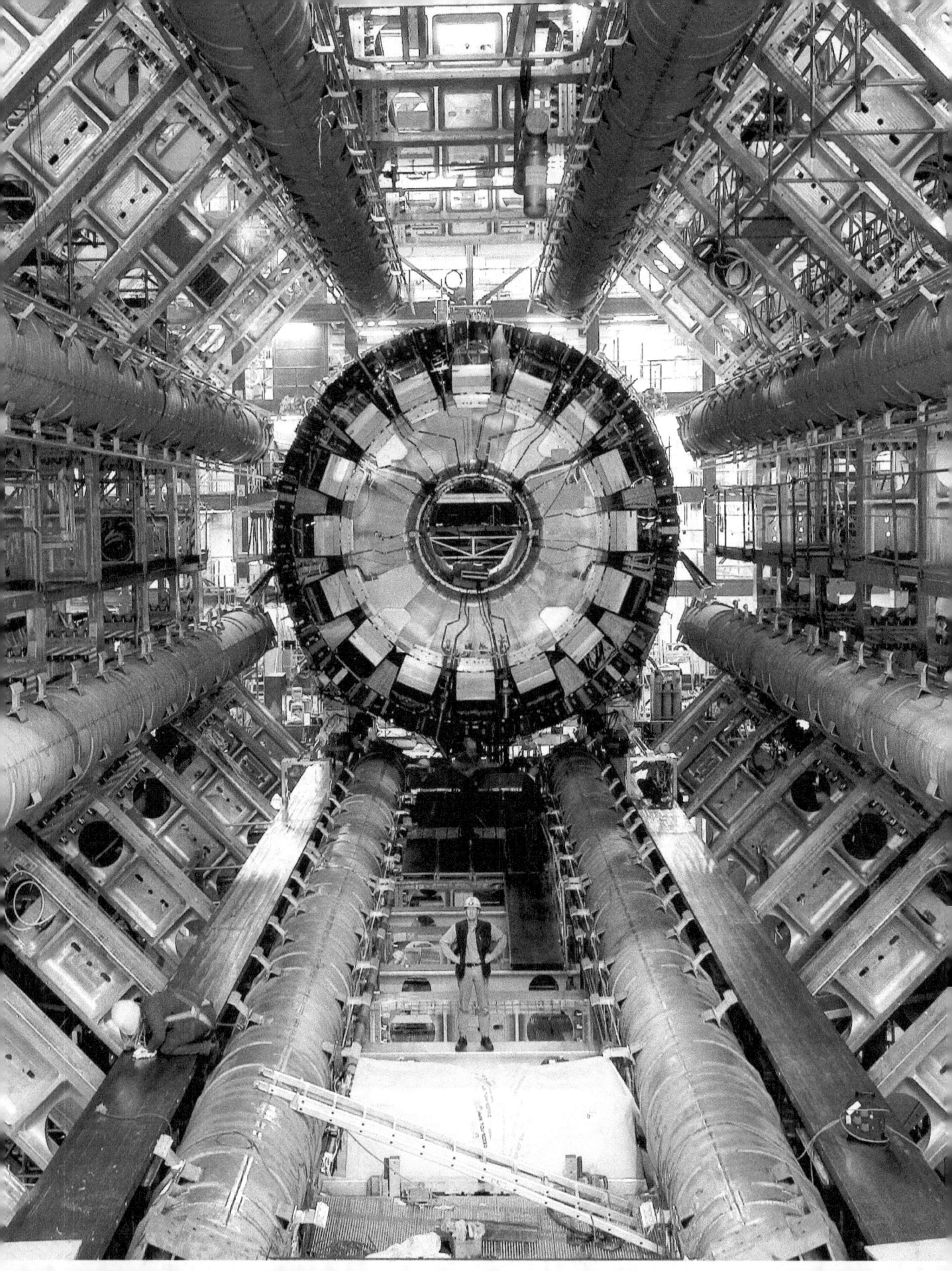

WE CREATE AND APPLY KNOWLEDGE

Minding the Matter

Students from the School of Physics are answering some of humanity's deepest existential questions. Where does matter come from? How is mass generated? Where lies the 'dark mass' (as yet undiscovered) matter? In so doing, they are leading scientific teams on the world's largest stages.

The eight toroid magnets can be seen surrounding the calorimeter that is later moved into the middle of the ATLAS detector. This calorimeter will measure the energies of particles produced when protons collide in the centre of the detector. Photo: Maximilien Brice, CERN

PHYSICS AND CERN

Wits is the single largest contributor of graduate students to the SA-European Council for Nuclear Research (in French, Conseil Européen pour la Recherche Nucléaire, or CERN) programme, providing about 60 postgraduate students and technical, research and academic staff. CERN hosts the most powerful particle accelerator in the world, the Large Hadron Collider, and its members achieved fame for contributing to the invention of the Internet and the discovery of the Higgs boson particle.

Wits Professor Bruce Mellado, director of the Wits Institute for Collider Particle Physics (ICPP) and a senior scientist at iThemba LABS, was a lead participant in the discovery of the Higgs boson at the ATLAS experiment. For over a decade, Mellado devised data analysis strategies that enabled the discovery.

THE FUTURE

Wits doctoral students in the School of Physics, Humphry Tlou (top) and Edward Nkadimeng (bottom), during their time at CERN in Geneva, Switzerland. Photos: Courtesy of Humphry Tlou and Edward Nkadimeng

'The School of Physics is developing high-level skills and graduates are in demand.' Professor Bruce Mellado

Some Witsies have taken on key leadership positions at the prestigious ICPP laboratory. Humphry Tlou is one such student. A second-year PhD student in the School of Physics, he is the co-ordinator of maintenance and operations at the ICPP. He was the recipient of the 2020 doctoral SA-CERN Excellence Scholarship and the prestigious 2020 ATLAS PhD grant, awarded to two of the 1 200 PhD students working on the ATLAS experiment. The grant aims to encourage and support high-calibre doctoral students in particle physics research from all over the world, allowing them to obtain world-class exposure, supervision and training within the ATLAS collaboration. 'I am excited to contribute more towards the research and advancement of technology,' says Tlou, who hails from a small town called Mokopane in Limpopo, South Africa.

Another Wits graduate, Edward Nkadimeng, a doctoral student in the school, has been appointed by the management of the ATLAS experiment at CERN to lead a community of physicists and engineers from 26 institutes from the United States and Europe. Nkadimeng was the recipient of the prestigious 2020 Southern African Institute for Nuclear Technology and Sciences fellowship from iThemba LABS of the National Research Foundation.

'These appointments are a demonstration of South Africa's ability to lead in top-notch international projects and are an epitome of world-class and inclusive excellence, where new scientists are being trained to become leaders,' says Mellado.

Wits' contribution covers all areas of activity of the SA-CERN programme: the ALICE (A Large Ion Collider Experiment), ATLAS and ISOLDE (Isotope mass Separator On-Line) experiments, and theory. Wits has a large involvement, in particular with the ATLAS experiment, which includes contributions to hardware instrumentation, firmware and software development, radiation certification, physics analysis, big data and artificial intelligence. The Wits ICPP leverages these activities to deliver world-class training to South African postgraduate students and to provide technology transfer to the country.

SCIENTIFIC SPIN-OFFS

South Africa's involvement at CERN is supported by the Department of Science and Innovation and the National Research Foundation. The SA-CERN programme, which was launched in 2008, has significantly increased the local and international footprint and visibility of South Africa in Big Science.

The CERN connection has had many spin-offs for the local science and technology industry. The team is expected to deliver critical electronics for the high-luminosity upgrade of the ATLAS detector. The Low Voltage Power Supply (LVPS) project will power the future of detector electronics in the presence of high radiation levels and is one of the components that is being redesigned. These electronics will be manufactured and assembled in South Africa. Another link is with the Square Kilometre Array (SKA) project. While the collider is the world's biggest microscope and SKA the largest telescope, both are looking for the origins of mass – CERN in the smallest particles and SKA in the furthest stars.

On a fundamental level, the discovery of the Higgs boson (and much of the work at CERN) involves working with big data. This knowledge of artificial intelligence combined with big data, and classical approaches to science, is being used to solve complex problems – for example, through modelling. During the coronavirus pandemic, Mellado worked with the Gauteng provincial government, IBM and other partners, and used artificial intelligence to model Covid-19 infection rates and hotspots.[19]

Wits Vice-Chancellor and Principal Zeblon Vilakazi is a physicist by training and is widely known as the 'father of SA-CERN'. As the director of iThemba LABS in 2008, he motivated for South Africa to be involved with CERN and was one of the first generation of African scientists at CERN, working on the electronics of the project (amongst other aspects).

THE FUTURE

Using MeerKAT, astronomers search for pulsars and map the hydrogen distribution, which gives them a great deal of information about the structure of the universe. Source: Courtesy of the South African Radio Astronomy Observatory

CREATING SCIENCE ECOSYSTEMS

International collaborations like CERN and the SKA are extremely important because they allow South African scientists to tap into huge areas of knowledge that can be used to solve complex problems. Mellado and his colleagues in Wits Physics are interested in creating science ecosystems where innovation flourishes. These comprehensive ecosystems see iThemba LABS, located on the Wits campus, and industry co-existing in the same space. 'We want to avoid the "ivory tower", and establish a nexus between fundamental science, academia and industry to allow for a much easier flow of information,' Mellado says. 'This is a paradigm shift because science is usually heavily regulated [being funded by government] and the pool of knowledge is only transmitted globally through articles and conferences.'

DEVELOPING EMPLOYABLE GRADUATES

From 2012 to the present, the number of South Africans working in cutting-edge physics has grown from a handful to well over 100. Key to this increase is creating interest in physics at the secondary school level in order to develop a flow of students from secondary to tertiary level studies. Mellado is passionate about identifying potential early and nurturing these students to become the next generation of leaders in science. 'How do we, as mature scientists, create a generation of leaders? How do we train leaders that transform society and science? We need to identify potential leaders at the undergraduate level.'

Not only does Wits Physics boast some of the brightest talent, but it is also one of the most

'We are showing the government the future of academics.' Professor Bruce Mellado

inclusive pools of scientists in the country. 'One of the great achievements of Wits is that our student body is a transformed representation of South Africa and is based on excellence,' adds Mellado. 'Edward [Nkadimeng, the lead scientist at ATLAS] does not come from a privileged background; however, these young scientists have natural intelligence – they are brilliant!'

The School of Physics is developing high-level skills and graduates are in demand. They are hired by some of the world's top consulting and engineering companies and nearly all of them find jobs. 'Our graduates enjoy full employment in South Africa,' says Mellado. 'While this is a sign of the success of our training programme, it depletes the pool of students that continue to conduct research.' In his view there are not enough PhD students. 'They need to see that there is a career path in academia. We need to leverage international collaborations to enhance the number of PhD students and ensure that they are groomed, mentored and cared for, and encouraged to pursue a science career.'

Until then, Wits Physics students will keep looking for the unknown – in the smallest and furthest spaces.

WITS FUTURISTS LEAD THE WAY: ACHILLE MBEMBE

The Future is African

He has studied at the Sorbonne in Paris, worked at Columbia and Pennsylvania universities, was a visiting professor at the universities of California, Yale, Duke and Harvard, and his books and essays have been translated into 15 languages.

Cameroonian philosopher, political theorist, and public intellectual, Wits Professor Achille Mbembe. His writing about contemporary African and global phenomena has positioned him as one of the most important public intellectuals in the world today. Photo: Yves Krier

Yet Achille Mbembe, research professor in history and politics at Wits, chooses to live in South Africa. 'Africa is a planetary laboratory,' he explains. 'If studied properly, it gives us signs of where the world is going. Before the end of this century, we'll have the youngest population on Earth, although this comes with numerous constraints and responsibilities. No continent can equal Africa in terms of our resilience and potential for innovation. In South Africa in particular, we enjoy an unparalleled extent of academic freedom. These are all vital resources and potentials that our universities should be using.'

'Only a university that emerges from the cauldron of this City, and embraces it, can produce what Wits has produced.' Professor Achille Mbembe

Mbembe is a leading academic and researcher in the fields of critical theory, African history, politics and social science, and is widely regarded as one of the most important public intellectuals writing about contemporary African and global phenomena in the world today.

He has been involved at the Wits Institute for Social and Economic Research (WiSER) since its inception in 2001. 'The institute was established to accompany the transition that the country was undergoing in the aftermath of apartheid. The aim was to become an intellectual hub in the Global South and the premier humanities research institute on the continent. I would argue that it's fulfilled that mission,' says Mbembe. A lot of work remains to be done – not only in South Africa but globally. 'No matter where you are, it's not easy to be a Black person today,' he says. 'The colour of your skin still penalises you. We must create a place on Earth where that's not the case. That place must be in Africa. We have a duty to our continent to make it hospitable to people of African origin no matter their nationality – and all good-willed people who would like to tie their fate to the fate of the continent. We need to invest in the intellectual work of the highest quality for this to happen.'

Mbembe believes that Wits is the place to do so. 'Wits' location in Johannesburg and in Gauteng, where most of the wealth but also most of the inequalities on the continent are concentrated, makes it a hot laboratory for this cultural, intellectual, social and economic project. Only a university that emerges from the cauldron of this City, and embraces it, can produce what Wits has produced.'

His current research, on 'life futures in the age of planetary change', has kept him occupied with the advent of the Anthropocene (the most recent geological time period). 'We're likely to meet the extreme limits of the Earth if we don't change our ways of relating to nature and the environment. I'm researching how we can engage in the work of repairing the planet, caring for it and sharing it. Our future on Earth depends on our capacity to strike a balance between us and every other living thing.'

Achille Mbembe has an A1 rating from the South African National Research Foundation and is a member of the American Academy of Arts and Sciences. He has received numerous awards – among them the Gerda Henkel Award (for excellent research in the historical humanities) and, in 2018, the Ernst Bloch Award (for his influence in the field of critical theory).

The Wits Institute for Social and Economic Research, currently led by Professor Sarah Nuttall, has established itself as the pre-eminent interdisciplinary research institute in the humanities and social sciences in South Africa, and as one of the most influential globally. Its objective is to 'foster independent, critical enquiry into the complexities and paradoxes of change in South Africa'.

In 2021, Professor Achille Mbembe was commissioned by the president of France to work with civil society and other African groups on an important report focusing on future relations between Africa and France.

WE HARNESS THE POWER OF PLACE

Fringe of the Future

It was the size of a large desk, required its own room and a special cooling plant, and had the capabilities of a high-end calculator. In 1960, the IBM Model 1620 Mark 1 was a marvel of modern technology – and Wits was the first South African university to own one.

Brandon Fisher and his colleague Mpho Makutu work on designs at the MakerSpace in the Tshimologong Digital Innovation Precinct in Braamfontein. Photo: Daniel Born

Nearly 60 years later, in 2019, Wits made headlines again when it became the first African partner on the IBM Q Network. Wits can access the 20-qubit-IBM Q quantum computer from its 'tech playground', Tshimologong, in Braamfontein. Though still in its infancy, the technology is expected to grow exponentially.

INNOVATION ECOSYSTEM

Tshimologong is a digital innovation precinct where programmers, designers, developers, entrepreneurs and start-ups have been gathering since 2016. It is open to University staff and students, as well as to the public, to encourage collaboration, creativity and entrepreneurship.

THE FUTURE

Dr Solomon Assefa from IBM (left) and Professor Zeblon Vilakazi from Wits University at the occasion marking the expansion of the IBM Quantum Computing Network into Africa, with Wits being the first African university to access a quantum computer. Photo: Erna van Wyk

This pioneering precinct is the brainchild of Emeritus Professor Barry Dwolatzky, director of Innovation Strategy at Wits and director of the Joburg Centre for Software Engineering (JCSE) hosted at Wits, to support the local software economy. 'The goals of the JCSE were skills development, to promote best practice and to build the ICT industry in South Africa,' says Dwolatzky. 'During my travels doing that work, I realised the importance of start-ups in innovation. Innovative ideas aren't born at big corporations. They're developed at hubs and incubators – like they were in the "mom and dad garages" in the days when Bill Gates started work at Microsoft and Steve Jobs at Apple.'

There were a few attempts to start such hubs around the country, but none were truly successful, which set Dwolatzky's mind wondering. 'I started thinking about how to create a viable digital incubator and innovation hub in Johannesburg, the business centre of Africa.' He identified several critical factors for success by visiting university-led incubation hubs around the world. 'Number one on the list was the location. It had to be in an existing business centre, with existing infrastructure, near a campus of a major research university, and in an area already frequented by young, innovative, dynamic people. Braamfontein ticked every one of those boxes,' says Dwolatzky.

At the time, the area was dilapidated and dangerous. 'I discovered that Wits owned many of those empty buildings. I was allowed to use them on condition that I raised all the funds for the renovations.' It was a monumental task – the buildings were falling apart, with rats and pigeons as occupants. 'But IBM came on board to host a research lab in one of the buildings. It would be only the 13th such laboratory in the world and the second in Africa (the other being in Kenya), and very prestigious. It was a massive coup!'

TECH TRIUMPH

The two-level, 900-square-metre IBM lab was completed in 2016 and the final building at Tshimologong was finished in 2017. The project has since drawn interest and funding from other sectors of society.

Tshimologong comprises several different spaces. The Coworking Space lets tech and digital entrepreneurs work together and practise peer-to-peer mentoring. The Incubator is a coaching hub for entrepreneurs. The Skills Academy teaches entry-level ICT skills and programming languages and has an Animation Development Academy, where graduates are upskilled to prepare for industry. The MakerSpace is built for the needs of rapid prototyping and robotics builders.

Tshimologong has made a name as a 24/7 tech hub where concepts come to fruition, and where the boundaries of possibility are constantly pushed. Looking back, Dwolatzky says that there were many highlights. 'One very successful event was the Hack Jozi Challenge, where the City put up R5 million in funding, including a R1 million prize for the winner, where any

'Innovative ideas aren't born at big corporations. They're developed at hubs and incubators.' Emeritus Professor Barry Dwolatzky

THE FUTURE

156

Professor Zeblon Vilakazi with innovators at the MakerSpace at the Tshimologong Digital Innovation Precinct in Braamfontein.
Source: Tshimologong, University of the Witwatersrand

Neo Hutiri, a Wits graduate, developed the 'Pelebox', a smart locker that cuts down queueing times for patients collecting chronic medication, which was named one of Time magazine's best inventions in 2019. Source: Tshimologong, University of the Witwatersrand

citizen could enter with ideas to improve the City. The winner, Neo Hutiri, a Wits engineering graduate, had a brilliant idea to dispense chronic medication. He designed smart lockers that could be placed around the City, filled, and accessed by users through a one-time PIN – saving them hours normally spent waiting in queues at public clinics. He was named one of *Time* magazine's top 100 innovators for the project.'

'Another fascinating project is Raptor, which uses machine learning to improve biometric facial recognition in Africa. These systems were mostly built abroad and programmed on Western faces, and Raptor aims to improve facial recognition here in Africa,' he adds.

'Our annual digital arts festival, Fak'ugesi, has grown exponentially and now incorporates gaming development, art, animation, music and more – it's become a beacon for the connected Braamfontein of the future.' Its current director, Dr Tegan Bristow, won a prestigious National Science and Technology Forum Award in 2021.

AFRICAN IMPACT

In 2019, Wits was the first African university to access IBM's quantum computers, hosted in New York, through the cloud. 'The next big drive is in quantum computing, which operates in the subatomic world, and which can theoretically solve problems that other computers can't – though it's still quite experimental at this stage,' says Dwolatzky. He is of the firm belief that Africa should be in on this action. 'South Africa isn't known as a big tech player, but I believe that we're just bad at telling our stories. There have been some amazing innovations and technologies in the country. Some of the research at Wits and Tshimologong blows my socks off. If we're going to be serious players in digital transformation, we need places like Tshimologong and the IBM lab – after that, it's just up to us to be ambitious.'

Dwolatzky's vision is not yet fully realised. His hope is that Braamfontein, not just Tshimologong, 'will become a cluster of innovation in the city, where major companies and start-ups open their doors, all feeding off each other and Wits – the way that Silicon Valley feeds off Stanford University in the US.'

If the precinct continues on its current trajectory, that may well be the case.

Normal computers use bits, while quantum computers use qubits. Bits are always either in an on or off position, while qubits can be on and off at the same time, or somewhere on the spectrum between – allowing for uncertainty. IBM uses the analogy of a piano: a normal computer plays one note at a time until it finds the correct answer to a question. A quantum computer can play two or more notes at the same time, delivering a new sound – and answers that not even the strongest supercomputers of today can find.

The School of Computer Science and Applied Mathematics at Wits has preserved the remnants of the IBM Model 1620 Mark 1, its first computer. It is housed, along with other old Wits computers, in the Computer Museum, which is part of the TW Kambule Mathematical Sciences Laboratory.

In June 2021, a Wits team competed in the RoboCup tournament, the World Cup for soccer robots, with the goal of advancing intelligent robots.

Tshimologong was registered as a separate commercial entity in 2017, though it is still wholly owned by Wits. Lesley Donna Williams, the appointed CEO, was a recipient of the 2018 InspiringFifty award, an initiative that recognises the 50 most inspiring women in South Africa's science, technology, engineering and mathematics industries.

In 2021, Byrne and his collaborators found that light pollution makes it difficult for dung beetles to see the stars, which they use to orientate. The team also determined that elevated carbon dioxide levels in the atmosphere negatively affect dung beetles' size and survival. Photo: Shivan Parusnath

WITS FUTURISTS LEAD THE WAY: MARCUS BYRNE

Dirty Science

'Today, I want to share my passion for poo with you,' begins Marcus Byrne, professor in the School of Animal, Plant and Environmental Sciences, in a TED Talk video that's been viewed over 1.1 million times.

Professor Byrne goes on to describe his extensive research on dung beetles, a topic that lends itself to a plethora of puns, and he soon has the audience in stitches. His team's biggest breakthrough was proving that dung beetles can navigate using the Milky Way – earning the team an Ig Nobel Prize in 2013. 'My dad, not knowing the difference, told everyone back home that we won a Nobel Prize. It even went into the local school magazine,' laughs Byrne.

'Dung beetles using the Milky Way to orientate themselves has profound implications for artificial intelligence.'
Professor Marcus Byrne

'I grew up wanting to be a biologist, with Sir David Attenborough as my hero, and completed my studies in the UK. When I came to South Africa, following a girlfriend, I got a job as a lab technician at the Australian Dung Beetle Research Unit in Pretoria. I'm British, so I was terrified of insects, but it soon dawned on me how fabulous these animals are.'

He later joined the Wits academic staff, teaching zoology and entomology. He's since researched how dung beetles orientate themselves in unknown environments, whether they can see polarised light, and how they keep cool while walking over hot sand – even fashioning little beetle boots out of a dental compound for the purpose. 'Really, we're just out there having a lot of fun,' Byrne chuckles, 'visiting beautiful places in the bush and making it up as we go along.'

The research has some profound implications, including for the fields of robotics and artificial intelligence. 'While humans can store a complex map of their surroundings in their brain, using landmarks as guides, dung beetles don't have the neural capabilities. They use external cues, such as the Milky Way, to orientate themselves. That's what you want in an autonomous vehicle – something that can go into unknown terrain and always orientate itself.'

Although Byrne's research focus is on the biological control of invasive plant species, he's earned an international reputation as a brilliant science communicator. 'I've learned that if you can make people laugh, it holds their attention,' he says. 'Of course, this doesn't work for every scientific topic, but I do think that science communication needs to change in some ways to engage the average person. Science often undermines culture and religion, and people will deny the cold, hard facts if it goes against their beliefs – look at climate-change deniers. Scientists need to be gentler on people's thoughts and ideas to convince them of the facts. Science, sometimes, needs to be a social issue.'

The humble dung beetle has taken Byrne all over the world to deliver talks on the topic. Three years ago, he finally got to meet his hero. 'David Attenborough did a programme about our research and I got to work with him for two days. He was a true gentleman and lived up to all my expectations. We were filming in the Bristol Planetarium in England and he finished off with the words: "Had the Egyptians known that this lowly animal could orientate using the centre of the galaxy, they would have been justified in having elevated it to the status of a god." It was a full-circle moment for me, and nearly brought me to tears.'

The Ig Nobel Prize, presented annually since 1991 at Harvard University in the US, recognises research that makes people 'laugh, then think'. It might be an inside joke in the academic community, but that doesn't mean the research isn't significant. The winner of the 2000 Ig Nobel Prize in Physics, for the magnetic levitation of a live frog, also won the actual 2010 Nobel Prize in Physics.

Byrne shares the Ig Nobel Prize, awarded jointly in the fields of biology and astronomy, with Marie Dacke, Emily Baird, Clarke Scholtz and Eric J. Warrant.

THE FUTURE

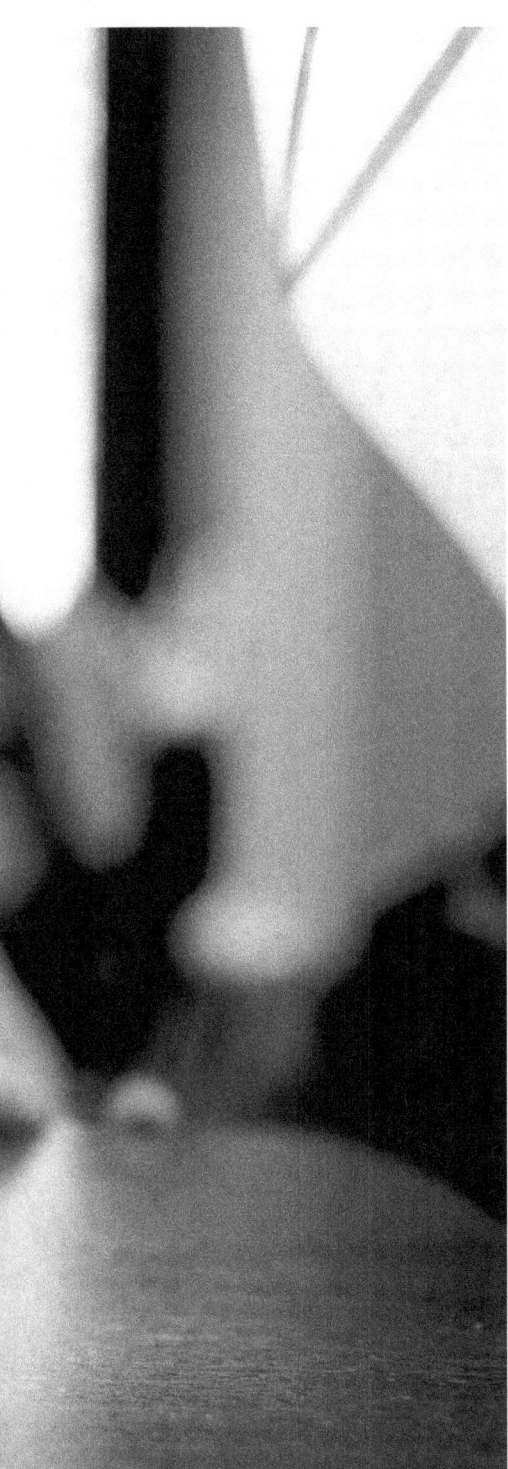

Professor Byrne displays a dung beetle in the Planetarium, soon to become the Wits Digital Dome. The star projector was used to determine whether the beetles navigated via the stars of the Milky Way galaxy. Photo: Chris Collingridge

The Cross Bearers *sculpture by Ernest Ullmann in front of the Rembrandt Building.*

Photo: Shivan Parusnath

WE ARE GLOBAL

African Art Beat: Wits Art Museum

The Wits Art Museum (WAM) opened its doors to the public in 2012 and has since become the leading museum of African art on the continent, housing around 15 000 artworks.

Exterior view of the Wits Art Museum, home to an extraordinary African art collection and a leading museum of contemporary and historical African art. Source: Wits Art Museum

A CONTINENT IN TECHNICOLOUR

As the first large art museum in South Africa dedicated to African art, the Wits Art Museum's cultural importance cannot be underestimated, says Julia Charlton, senior curator. 'Some of the works include masks, staffs, stools, pipes, snuff containers, textiles, tapestries and beadwork. The collection is extremely diverse and reflects the multiple art forms produced across the continent.'

'One of our aims when selecting artworks is to showcase artists who didn't get the recognition they deserved in their lifetime, whether because of apartheid or because of prejudice around what constitutes art and what is worth studying,' she adds.

THE FUTURE

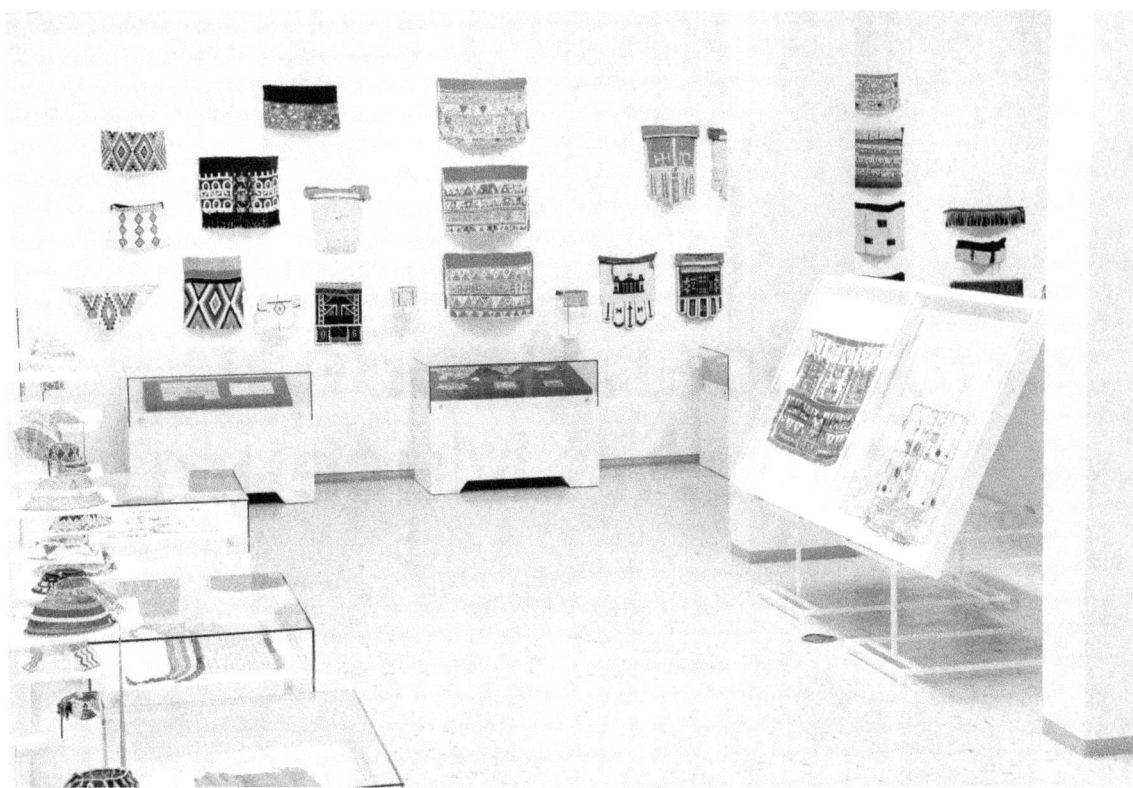

The Beadwork, Art and the Body *exhibition held at the WAM showcased a dazzling range of African beadwork. Source: Wits Art Museum*

Tropical Love Storm by William Kentridge, *1985. Charcoal and crayon on paper, 985 mm x 690 mm, Wits Art Museum. Acquired 1985. Source: Courtesy of the artist*

Alongside these works, the museum also has thousands of works in more traditional media such as photographs, paintings, sculptures, etchings and drawings. On one occasion, a global artist made it onto the programme – the opening of an Andy Warhol exhibition in 2017 drew 5 000 visitors. 'It was wild!' beams Charlton. 'The museum was absolutely pumping that night.'

Another big drawcard was a 2013 exhibition of Gerard Sekoto's work. 'He has this iconic status as an African painter who recorded life in townships, as well as his experiences in Senegal and Paris during his self-imposed exile. He's one of the pioneers of modern South African art.'

Charlton's personal favourites are the exhibitions that touch hearts and minds. 'Zanele Muholi, who identifies as an "artivist" for the LGBTQIA+ community, did amazing portraits of people who live their truth despite the dangers of doing so in townships. It was powerful opening that exhibition here in 2014 and seeing how art can make a difference in people's lives.'

The museum is planning an exhibition in 2022 to showcase female artists who have historically been neglected in the arts. 'The collections include a large body of work by women in art forms that have previously been denied the status of art. I'm proud that we're able to use our resources for the public good,' says Charlton.

'As a public-facing university museum, accessibility is key. We do not charge an entrance fee because these amazing art collections should be open to everybody, not just the University.' Julia Charlton

FROM PIONEERS TO PRESENT DAY

The University has been collecting African art since 1930, first through the Department of Anthropology and later as part of teaching collections in fine arts and architecture.

The museum's partnership with Standard Bank in 1979 was a breakthrough. The Standard Bank African Art Collection, funded by an annual purchasing grant over the last 40 years, contains over 5 000 objects from across the continent. The wealth of knowledge of African art grew at Wits, which formed the first local Art History Department to introduce courses in African art into the curriculum, which helps inform curation.

Were it not for substantial donations over the years, including those from private individuals, the museum might not have been established, says Charlton. 'It took almost ten years, from fundraising to building, to open the museum. We couldn't have done it without our donors.'

Today the museum houses works by prominent South African artists, including paintings by Irma Stern, David Koloane and Judith Mason; pencil drawings by Gerard Sekoto; watercolours by Durant Sihlali; linocuts by John Muafangejo; bronze sculptures by Sydney

Kumalo and Edoardo Villa; and a large archive of work by Walter Battiss – to name a few.

Artists like William Kentridge, Robert Hodgins and David Goldblatt have been generous with their donations to the museum over the years. Jack Ginsberg, a Wits graduate, donated a massive collection of works recently. The Jack Ginsberg Centre for Book Arts opened in 2019, with over 3 000 artists' books. An artist's book, explains Charlton, is a new art form. 'The defining characteristic of these works is that they can be held or engaged with in some way. Some are literal books created by the artists, while others are conceptual pieces that challenge the conventional book format.

An interesting item in the collection is Pippa Skotnes' horse skeleton with the text inscribed on the bones. Another is a piece of felt; another is wrapped in barbed wire. The collection at the WAM is the biggest in the Southern Hemisphere.'

ART ON DEMAND

Public spaces like the Wits Art Museum matter, says Charlton. 'As a public-facing university museum, accessibility is key. We do not charge an entrance fee because these amazing art collections should be open to everybody, not just the University. We also run extensive education and events programmes in addition to our exhibitions.'

Visitors consider Pippa Skotnes' literary horse book art at the launch of the Jack Ginsberg Centre for Book Arts. Source: Wits Art Museum

The location was important to this vision, she adds. 'The museum was designed to be part of the City's cultural arc, but on the edge of campus. We have a corner café where refreshments are served at openings and the crowd flows onto the street, immersed in the City.'

Striking a balance between academic and public needs is key to the museum's success. Students research the artworks and get published in art catalogues, while collaborations with several University departments have led to powerful exhibitions and teaching opportunities. Students have also produced creative additions to some of the artworks over the years. Postgraduate music student Yonela Mnana created a jazz score to accompany an artwork. A group of postgraduate digital arts students collaborated to create new art that interacted with traditional masks. 'One notable example was a rig built around a mask that was originally not created for public view. When visitors ventured too close, curtains would cover the mask.'

The museum plans to extend its exhibitions beyond its physical borders through webinars and other digital platforms. 'We know that this is essential in attracting newer generations,' says Charlton. 'But it will always be a combination as we try to attract visitors into the museum. Art is most powerful when you are physically around it. As staff, we are happiest when hearing the voices of visitors float up to our office space from downstairs.'

A national competition was held to solicit design proposals for the Wits Art Museum. In 2012, the winning team, architects and Wits alumnae Nina Cohen and Fiona Garson, were awarded the Visi magazine's Architecture Award for their work.

The Wits Art Museum is situated in the heart of buzzing Braamfontein, a stone's throw from the Nelson Mandela Bridge. Its five floors across three buildings host five gallery spaces, offices and state-of-the-art storage facilities. The free access and a dynamic public exhibition and education programme make it a drawcard to local as well as international visitors.

The Andy Warhol exhibition was made possible by the Bank of America and Merrill Lynch SA. The bank continues to support the museum's education programme.

The museum is part of Wits' cultural and arts space, located close to the Wits Theatre Complex, the revamped Wits School of Arts and the new Chris Seabrooke Music Hall.

I Have a Dream ...

Four members of the 2020/2021 Students' Representative Council weigh in on their hopes for Wits University at 100 years and beyond.

MPENDULO MFEKA: PRESIDENT (LLB)
As a keen chess player and fiction fiend, Mfeka might seem reserved. But he harbours a fiery passion for the betterment of society.

Why Wits? Wits was a dream for me. I've seen the places that it can take its graduates. That's also why I wanted to be on the SRC – education is so important and everyone should have that opportunity. I want to do my part to make education accessible to everyone, especially the underprivileged.

What should every student know? No matter where you're from, always strive to be better. If you work hard and believe in yourself, anything is possible. Remember to empower those around you as you improve yourself.

Mpendulo Mfeka, president of the 2020/21 Wits Students' Representative Council (SRC). Photo: Daniel Born

SPHESIHLE MNDZEBELE: PROJECTS, MEDIA, CAMPAIGNS AND STUDENT ENTREPRENEURSHIP PORTFOLIO (BSC CONSTRUCTION)
As an Eswatini native, self-proclaimed feminist and avid soccer player, Mndzebele always wanted to be a Witsie.

Why did you want to be on the SRC? I believe in equality and I'm a humanitarian by nature. I wanted to help, to represent those who don't have a voice.

What is your vision of a future Wits? An institution where exclusion doesn't exist, whether academic or financial, because free education has become the human right people say it is. Students can learn in their native language, and there are more women in positions of power.

Wits SRC member Sphesihle Mndzebele. Photo: Daniel Born

In February 2022, Wits SRC President Cebolenkosi Khumalo and comrades walked from the Wits Great Hall to the Union Buildings in Pretoria, and raised R6 million in student funding. This amount was matched by the University to enable access for students to Wits.

The SRC accumulated a large collection of material not readily available through conventional avenues – including material produced by anti-apartheid organisations. This valuable collection was eventually housed in the Wits SRC Resource Centre, established in late 1980. In 1984, the Resource Centre was destroyed in a fire that was later confirmed as arson.

Student organisations such as the SRC have an important political role to play in society. Wits and its students mobilised opposition against apartheid, staging several protests against academic segregation. These culminated in attacks on Wits demonstrators by the police force and the arrest of the SRC president in 1969, while the 1971 SRC president was deported.

In the lead-up to Wits' centennial, a former Wits SRC president, Rex Heinke, pledged $100 000 to aid students and challenged other former SRC leaders to contribute: 'Wits needs your help now to build a new generation of South African leaders to fulfil the dream of a free and democratic South Africa.' Heinke's contribution will be channelled towards the Wits Food Bank and the Wits Covid-19 Relief Fund. The Wits Food Bank, established in 2013, assists approximately 5 000 students per year.

'Campus life changes you. Let it.' Lesego Makinita

LESEGO MAKINITA: GENDER AND TRANSFORMATION PORTFOLIO (BED)

Makinita is a social animal who spends his days on the streets of Braamfontein, taking pictures and chatting with fellow students.

What has Wits taught you? Campus life changes you – so many new perspectives and backgrounds will shake you up. Let it. Change challenges you and shapes you for the better.

What needs to change on campus? As a member of the LGBTQIA+ community, I want to see an end to discrimination and marginalisation of all kinds. To do that, we need to speak up and educate people. Knowledge and familiarity can help break stigma.

Wits SRC member Lesego Makinita. Photo: Daniel Born

GABRIELLA FARBER: LEGAL, POLICY, GOVERNANCE AND HEALTH PORTFOLIO (BA LAW AND INTERNATIONAL RELATIONS)

During her first lecture at Wits, a campus protest opened Farber's eyes to her 'sheltered upbringing'. She knew she needed to add her voice.

What issues are students facing today? As we ride out the pandemic, mental health issues are taking their toll. I want other students to know that it's not a weakness; there is strength in accepting and embracing these problems.

Where will Wits be 50 years from now? I hope that education will be free for everyone. But there is work to be done – change doesn't start in government boardrooms; it starts on the ground. Students need to realise that if one of us suffers, everyone does. Step up and join the fight, no matter your background, colour or creed. If you're privileged, use that position to help others.

Wits SRC member Gabriella Farber. Photo: Daniel Born

Photo: Shivan Parushath

Photo: Peter Maher

The Next Century Begins Now

The earth will swallow us who burrow
And, if I die there underground,
What does it matter? Who am I?
Dear Lord! all round me every day,
I see men stumble, fall and die.

Benedict Vilakazi, 'In the Gold Mines'

Reflecting on the ten decades of Wits University's existence, and using the memory-jog of the timeline included in this book, it is worth pausing for a moment on the threshold of Wits' new century to look with fresh eyes on the City that embraced the University and grew alongside it. At its inception, Wits responded to its time, providing research into technology and support for the nascent gold-mining industry, which, although unevenly shared, was the foundation of the South African economy. Vilakazi's powerful poem reminds us of the back-breaking labour of the countless unacknowledged miners who risked their lives for little reward and whose access to much of what the City offered was barred. Their unheard voice is acknowledged in a plaque outside the Enoch Sontonga entrance to Braamfontein Campus West, which commemorated the march of 7 000 mine workers who walked from Johannesburg to KwaZulu-Natal as part of a national protest in 1899.

Over time the University found its own, independent voice and used that voice to good effect, standing firm by its principles of academic freedom in the face of a government that proposed that freedom was a 'whites-only' terrain.

As we have described in each of the previous chapters, historically, futuristically and thematically, and as we have also seen through the eyes of those who were early witnesses, Johannesburg is still there. It may not look the same, but it is not yet a physical, archaeological dig site for students looking for clues and messages from the past. And yet Johannesburg offers us an extraordinary laboratory for research and teaching. Wits is well positioned to continue its pioneering work of breaking new intellectual ground and reimagining a future that offers hope for humanity.

The nature and the scale of the challenges facing the City compel the University to engage with its urban environment. It is both fitting and appropriate that it should

The protest by Wits students and staff during the trial of Glenn Moss and four others on charges of contravening the Suppression of Communism Act 44 of 1950 revealed the rising student awareness of racial politics. Source: University of the Witwatersrand's Central Records Office and Archives

do so – through knowledge creation, intellectual critique, teaching programmes and the advancement of the public good. In fact, urban-related research has become a specialisation for Wits, and partnerships with government and other institutions on matters relating to urban development have been formed and are bearing fruit.

With an increasingly diverse and cosmopolitan urban society, including migrants from the rest of South Africa and the world, the complexity of the City presents many challenges. Cities of migrants are often associated with cultural, economic and intellectual innovation, but they can also be places of tension. Issues of xenophobia and migrant vulnerability need to be constantly addressed and confronted in constructive ways.

Hannelie Coetzee's hair-raising mural standing at 168 metres in Braamfontein is a reference to the idea of inclusivity. Partly inspired by a Wits graduate student's thesis, the work also references the ways in which different generations reflect upon themselves and reconfigure their own identities in relation to history. Photo: Daniel Born

Johannesburg is one of the most unequal cities in the world. More than three million of its residents experience economic deprivation. With its sprawling and fragmented urban footprint, it is also one of the world's most energy-inefficient cities. There are no easy solutions to many of these pressing concerns, but it is precisely because of these challenges and requirements that a complex urban context like the City is an excellent location for Wits. As a leading university, it is also well positioned for constructive debate concerning city development and urbanisation, and can provide a high level of academic expertise on urban challenges, not just locally, but more broadly from the perspective of the Global South.

As Wits looks forward to the next 100 years, it can be proud of standing strong in society. As the University is poised to advance further, a moment's pause to reflect is also necessary.

Wits is a premier university, ranked in the top one per cent in the world from amongst approximately 25 000 universities. The University's strategic objective to create an enabling environment for a research-intensive and postgraduate-oriented university is being realised. This includes achieving, since 2013, one of the fastest growth rates in research outputs submitted to the Department of Higher Education and Training, resulting in substantially increased research income received from the state. The number of postgraduate students has also increased to almost 40 per cent of the student body, in line with the University's vision.

The vision for 'where to from here' for Wits, as a university with both an African and a global footprint, is to continue in its rich tradition of knowledge generation and dissemination in different areas of endeavour. Producing graduates who are highly influential in global civil society is a core aim. In order to hold good on this promise, the University intends to continue to attract the best academics and students by demonstrating that Wits is their university of choice.

TOWARDS 2033

As a vital first step into its next century, Wits is in the process of developing its strategic plan for 2023 to 2033, building on its first 100 years of achievement and success.

The University's core purpose is to make a positive impact on society through creating and advancing global knowledge and fostering graduates to become leaders with integrity. Its vision is to produce socially responsive, highly adaptable, resilient graduates who can meet the challenges of a world changing more rapidly than ever before, and to serve as a hub of knowledge on the African continent in the drive to create inclusive and sustainable futures for all.

It will be important to provide an inclusive student experience that fosters a sense of belonging and that helps scholars to become active citizens and ethical, accountable leaders, no matter their role in society after graduation.

There will be no compromise on academic excellence and the standard of education on offer. This will require the ongoing use of the best pedagogies and technologies available in a multidisciplinary, flexible, academic environment. In order to enable access to higher education, Wits' academic offering is likely to expand to provide adaptable lifelong learning opportunities – for example, through online teaching and learning, and through offering micro and stackable credentials.

Research that advances the scientific, cultural, social and economic development of society, both local and global, is a further priority for the next decade. The University will expand research leadership; encourage trans-, cross- and multidisciplinary work; and build capacity. It will seek to build a pipeline of talented academic scholars, starting at the postgraduate and postdoctoral levels. It will also seek to incentivise researchers and scholars by according due recognition to impactful research endeavours. In support of innovation and entrepreneurship, Wits will also create the opportunities and processes needed for transforming research findings into marketable products.

Wits is well located to build innovative partnerships across sectors, and to develop local communities through its urban and rural campuses.

In all of its academic and research endeavours, Wits will continue to be guided by its commitment to social justice, to serve as an agent for change, to leverage its knowledge to address social issues within a context of equality and transparency, and to tackle future challenges from the perspective of the Global South. In its commitment to ecological justice, the University will seek to transform its campuses into a model for energy, water and waste efficiency; to improve access and safety; and to use new digital technologies to create modern, model campus environments that are conducive to learning.

If, by 2033, students, staff and alumni feel a sense of belonging and pride, if the university reflects the diversity of our country and continent, if professional, operational, and administration services are fully integrated to produce academic excellence, if Wits academics remain leading voices on issues relating to social advancement both in South Africa and beyond, and if the curriculum meets the changing needs of our society, the University will have achieved its first milestone in making its second century as successful as the first.

NEW ERA, NEW LEADERSHIP

Professor Zeblon Vilakazi was installed as the sixteenth vice-chancellor and principal of Wits University in April 2021. He had previously served as the vice-principal and deputy vice-chancellor for research and postgraduate affairs. Under his leadership, Wits' research output more than doubled, catapulting the University in the global university rankings.

Born in Katlehong on the East Rand, Vilakazi, a nuclear physicist, obtained his PhD from Wits in 1998. Globally recognised for his expert knowledge in physics and nuclear research, he was instrumental in establishing South Africa's first experimental high-energy physics research group at CERN, working on the Large Hadron Collider.

Vilakazi is tasked with leading the University into the next century.

'It's crucial for Wits' development and growth that we continue to develop local and global partnerships that cement the University's

Vice-Chancellor and Principal Zeblon Vilakazi at a graduation ceremony in 2020. Photo: Shivan Parusnath

position as a leader in innovation,' says Vilakazi. This includes ensuring that Wits and other African universities can access quantum computing facilities, something that Vilakazi has ensured through a partnership with IBM.

Reflecting on the University as a leader of social change for good, Vilakazi says: 'The watershed moment of our University's centennial year offers us an opportunity to build on the successes of our past, to value our current work and to shape tomorrow. I believe that there are three core areas that we will maintain as Wits transitions into its next century: developing excellent graduates who leave their mark on society; conducting world-class research and fostering innovation; and using our location in the economic heartland of Africa to lead from the Global South. Wits must be at the forefront of developing graduates who will find solutions to the pressing problems of the twenty-first century, some of which are still unknown. This will require us to further promote integration across disciplines and entrench continuous learning.'

'The recent pandemic disrupted how we teach and learn, but we should view this as an opportunity to harness digital transformation, not only in being at the cutting edge of excellence in teaching and learning, but also to address how we have overcome the digital divides of our society. We have the opportunity to become a centre for innovation and a hub for collaboration and partnership between key role players in industry and civil society. There are many examples where the University can become an important generator of patents, intellectual property, knowledge capital and technological innovation.'

'For a hundred years Wits has played a vital role in shaping our City and nation by addressing current challenges and innovating for our future,' he adds. 'We must leverage this past and our location to develop Wits as one of the leading research and innovation hubs in the world. We need to nurture the next generation of scholars and develop a talent pipeline par excellence. We must channel our knowledge and scholarship into innovative technologies, use it to influence policy, and above all ensure that it advances the public good.'

In considering the University's future, Vilakazi draws a direct link to its past and its origins: 'We should celebrate that which is unique about Wits. It was founded on protest against injustice and in support of academic freedom – as Jan Hofmeyr's inaugural address in 1922 bears witness. The University was born out of protest and the struggle to be recognised as a university in good standing when the dominant mining industry was reluctant to establish such an institution in a "rough and ready" town. Wits didn't take the tried and tested route of originating in a city guild or out of a religious institution. It was born of industry. The willingness to protest in defence of principles is in the Wits DNA and has been since the beginning.'

Wits invites you to celebrate 100 years of success and to be part of its next century. This invitation goes out to staff, students, alumni, collaborators, partners in research and innovation, funders, and friends who are interested in how a university that started in a mining town can bring its innate sense of innovation to unearth new possibilities in the city that adopted it, the continent that raised it and the world that has embraced it.

AFTERWORD

Universities enjoy longevity in society, akin to libraries and museums – they are institutions that usually outlast multiple generations; they serve as catalysts for the creation of new knowledge, as hubs for the preservation of societal memory over time and transform society for good.

Our universities provide a platform for new knowledge creation, for the development of high-level, scarce skills and for diverse ideas to be shared and exchanged in a safe space. They are also treasure troves of knowledge and need to be protected, valued, guarded and strengthened.

In times of disruption, we need strong public institutions – including universities – to remain steadfast, to uphold justice, to speak truth to power, to uplift humanity, and not to buckle in the face of challenges or threats from other sectors of society. Wits University has remained true to its values for one hundred years, despite the many societal and contextual challenges that it has navigated.

Photo: Shivan Parusnath

Research-intensive universities like Wits have a considered role to play in society – both as a catalyst for change and as a common facilitator for the exchange of ideas across disciplines, institutions, and indeed sectors, in order to gather the best expertise and experience to enable meaningful change in society.

Looking ahead, these universities should strive to create new knowledge and apply this knowledge for the benefit of society. Their research should enable the creation of innovative technologies that will impact on society for good.

Universities such as Wits are also well placed to replicate the high-level skills required, in adequate measure, to move South Africa forward. A wellspring of talent concentrated in a common physical or virtual space attracts further talent – smart people want to collaborate with other smart people. However, it is only at universities where specialists from multiple disciplines can congregate in a common space, draw on experts from other areas, and apply their minds to solve the complex 'glocal' challenges of our time.

Wits University embodies all the characteristics of a great university – it has an abundance of talented scholars and enthusiastic students who want to change the world for the better. It stands on the shoulders of over 200 000 illustrious alumni around the world who have the capability to transform society. It has the ability and credibility to serve as a nexus for the exchange of diverse ideas among diverse people and organisations in a changing world. It is well placed to continue its strong research trajectory, to continue with its discovery research, to impact on policy and society through its applied research and to spawn innovation that solves real-world problems.

We must focus on developing academically excellent graduates who leave their mark on society; we must continue to conduct world-class research and foster innovation and entrepreneurship; and we must use our location in the economic heartland of Africa to lead from the Global South.

We must develop ethical graduates with a keen sense of civic responsibility. Our polarised world is facing unprecedented challenges and we need to develop brave, principled, formidable graduates to meet these challenges.

We must be the place where thousands of exceptionally talented young individuals from all backgrounds can strive for excellence and emerge as leaders who will impact positively on society.

We must continue to take people from different ideologies, races, religions, cultures, classes and genders, and transform them into active global citizens who are equipped to deal with the complexities of this world – citizens who break away from their narrow enclaves, citizens who inspire others, citizens who create hope and go beyond what is possible. We must continue with this tradition and push beyond our latitudes if we are to succeed in the next one hundred years.

We need to move with the times but remain true to our core academic business of producing the next generation of leaders and knowledge that will create the world we want to live in. We need to be ready to adapt and embrace change to stay ahead of the curve.

We must aspire to create the African academy of the future. I believe that in the decades to come, Wits will continue to produce Nobel-prize-winning research. Africa needs to produce her own scholars who understand and can leverage the local context to contribute original knowledge to the global academy. We must create our own pipeline of academics so that we develop the next generation of scholars who excel in their disciplines, and who bring our unique, diverse backgrounds, contexts and knowledge to the global academy.

Finally, we must create an enabling environment for the flourishing of great ideas that will herald this continent into an era of innovation, change and growth for the next one hundred years.

Professor Zeblon Vilakazi

Vice-Chancellor and Principal of the University of the Witwatersrand, Johannesburg

ACKNOWLEDGEMENTS

The celebration of 100 years of excellence at Wits University has entailed the generous inputs of more people than we can thank here. Nonetheless, we wish in particular to acknowledge the Wits chancellor, Dr Judy Dlamini; the vice-chancellor and principal, Professor Zeblon Vilakazi; and the academics, researchers, staff and students who shared their stories so freely.

In addition, we are grateful to all the members of the Advancement Division who contributed in multiple ways to this extraordinary book; to the Wits Central Records Office and Wits Historical Papers for their extensive assistance in helping us source the archival material needed to produce this book. Roth Communications created the conceptual framework for the book and we thank them for their research and writing contribution. Special thanks are extended to Dr Shivan Parusnath, who provided many of the images that bring Wits alive to the reader. Finally, we are grateful to Jignasa Diar who designed the historic cover, Karen Lilje of Hybrid Creative for the book design, Inga Norenius who managed the production process and, ultimately, to Wits University Press for undertaking to publish *Wits University at 100*.

TIMELINE

Take a journey through Wits' history as it celebrates its centennial in 2022.

Early history

1896: The South African School of Mines is established in Kimberley.

1904: The Transvaal Technical Institute opens in Johannesburg as an extension of the South African School of Mines.

1906: The Transvaal Technical Institute is renamed the Transvaal University College.

1910: The college is renamed the South African School of Mines and Technology.

1920s

1920: The entity changes its name to the University College, Johannesburg.

1921: The Wits University Football Club is established. It remains one of the largest football clubs in South Africa today, training over 2 000 members in 2022.

1922: Full university status is granted, incorporating the college as the University of the Witwatersrand, with effect from 1 March. The University is inaugurated on 4 October. Prince Arthur of Connaught, governor-general of the Union of South Africa, becomes the University's first chancellor, and Professor Jan H Hofmeyr its first principal. Building begins at Milner Park on a site donated by the Johannesburg municipality.

1923: The University gradually vacates its premises in Eloff Street to move to the first completed teaching buildings at Milner Park (the Botany and Zoology block housing the departments of Geology, Botany, Zoology and Applied Mathematics). The University has six faculties (Arts, Science, Medicine, Engineering, Law and Commerce), 37 departments, 73 members of academic staff and a little more than 1 000 students. Wits University Press, the publisher of this book and a wealth of other academic texts, is established.

1925: The Prince of Wales officially opens Central Block.

1930s

1930: The Champion Tree, a eucalyptus (blue gum) tree with a massive crown, is planted, and today shades part of the Gavin Relly Green on West Campus.

1934: The University's first library opens on 12 March with book donations from private individuals, scientific societies, and institutions in the United States and Canada.

1935: Wits appoints its first Black staff member, Dr Benedict W Vilakazi, who publishes the first Zulu-English dictionary with Professor Clement Doke, a lecturer in the Department of Bantu Studies. Vilakazi Street in Soweto, where Wits alumnus and former South African president Nelson Mandela and Archbishop Desmond Tutu lived, is subsequently named in honour of Dr Vilakazi.

1936: Wits opens its first research institute, the Bernard Price Geophysical Research Institute, funded and donated by Dr Bernard Price. Important research on lightning and seismology is developed in the institute. The Special Radar Unit of the Corps of Signals, under Brigadier Basil Schonland, develops and builds equipment, and operates all South African radar activity from this institute.

1939: 2 544 students are enrolled.

1940s

1940: The Great Hall opens. Originally, the Central Block building was the unfinished façade of a two-storey wood and iron structure. Building was delayed by financial constraints but was finally completed in May 1940. In June, the governor-general officially opens the Wits Great Hall.

1943: The first major protest by Wits students against fee increases takes place, which sets the tone for student protests throughout the following decades.

1945: Student numbers grow to 3 100. The sudden increase in student enrolment after the Second World War leads to accommodation problems, which is temporarily resolved by the construction of wood and galvanised-iron hutments in the centre of the campus. These huts remained in use until 1972.

1946: Drs Donald Moikangoa and James Njongwe become the first Black doctors to graduate from the Wits Medical School. The first Black female doctor, Dr Mary Susan Malahlela-Xakana, graduated the following year.

1948: The National Party comes into power. Various student organisations become involved in the anti-apartheid movement.

1949: The Wits Convocation approves the first African medical scholarships after the Students' Representative Council requests that a fund be set up to support African students wishing to study medicine. This is a response to the government's move stopping all bursaries to African students eligible to study medicine, and confining medical training facilities for Black students to the University of Natal.

1950s

1951: The number of qualifications awarded by Wits reaches 10 433.

1954: Wits Convocation registers its strong protest against apartheid at a special general meeting on 23 February. It takes exception to the appointment of a government commission to investigate the 'practicability and financial implications of providing separate training facilities for Black students at the universities'.

1956: Wits Convocation Committee opposes segregation at universities. Convocation supports the Council, Senate, staff and students with regard to retaining its institutional autonomy and academic freedom.

1957: Two thousand students and staff members march to the Johannesburg City Hall behind the banner 'Against Separate Universities Bill'.

1959: The apartheid government passes the Extension of University Education Act, which enforces racial segregation in South African universities and bars all Black students from attending major universities in the country. Most affected are the four English-medium and liberal universities: Wits, Cape Town, Rhodes and the University of Natal. The University stages a protest in opposition to the new legislation, and students and staff line the streets of Johannesburg calling for government to end its interference in academic matters. Over the years, Wits maintains a firm, consistent and vigorous stand against apartheid, and protests continue. The consequences for the University are severe: banning, the detention and deportation of students and staff, and invasions of the campus by riot police to disrupt peaceful protest meetings. Also in 1959, *King Kong*, a landmark South African jazz musical, holds its opening at Wits University. It goes on to tour the country over the next two years and plays to multiracial audiences. The John Moffat Building opens and is named after Moffat, who bequeathed the greater part of his estate to Wits with the condition that something permanent be constructed.

1960s

1960: Wits acquires the Sterkfontein farm from the Stegmann family in this decade, with its world-famous limestone caves rich in archaeological material. The Planetarium opens on 12 October, the first in Africa and the second in the Southern Hemisphere.

1961: *The Unknown Miner*, a bronze statue, is sculpted by Herman Wald in honour of the thousands of migrant Black mine workers who worked on the gold mines of the Reef. The Atlas-like figure appears to hold up the rock surrounding the stopes deep beneath the surface and, in so doing, the whole edifice of mining. A similar sculpture is donated to Wits by Louis Wald in 2012, when the University celebrates its 90th birthday. Wits acquires a cheap, small nuclear reactor from a lab linked to Cambridge University, the alma mater of Professor Friedel Sellschop. The reactor is housed in the Nuclear Physics Research Unit and is key to the success of an international team, including Sellschop, devoted to the detection of neutrinos found in nature.

1962: Wits becomes the first university in the country to own a computer. Aside from a machine owned by the Council for Scientific and Industrial Research (CSIR), it is the only other scientific computer in the country. The computer is replaced with more advanced ones over the next decades and Wits maintains its leadership position in the computing field.

1963: Wits is home to 6 275 students.

1964: The medical library and the administrative offices of the Faculty of Medicine move to a new building in Esselen Street, Hillbrow. The Student Union opens on the Braamfontein Campus East after many years of deliberation about a suitable site. It is now a hub for student life and interaction, houses a mini student shopping mall called The Matrix, serves as the home of the Students' Representative Council, and is the centre of student clubs and organisations.

1966: Robert Kennedy visits Wits and makes a seminal speech against the apartheid government to a packed mixed audience in the Great Hall, saying: 'So many of these I have seen, so many who are in this hall, are standing with their brothers around the globe for liberty and equality and human dignity; not in the ease and comfort and approbation of society, but in midst of controversy and difficulty and risk.'

1968: The Graduate School of Business (Wits Business School) is established in Parktown. Today, it boasts an extensive management library, 24-hour meeting rooms and Africa's largest Case Study Centre, housing over 200 real-life cases that bring relevant business challenges into the classroom. Wits buys the Swartkrans farm, a source of archaeological material. The University also acquires excavation rights in caves of archaeological and palaeontological importance at Makapansgat in Limpopo.

1969: The Ernest Oppenheimer Residence is formally opened in Parktown. Savernake, the official residence of the vice-chancellor, located in Parktown, is made available to the University. The clinical departments in the new Medical School are opened.

1970s

1971: Wits hosts the first Free People's Concert, where performing alumni include Johnny Clegg and Des and Dawn Lindberg. These concerts continue through to the 1980s at various iconic venues including the Wits Library Lawns. It is one of the very few places where mixed races and bands come together.

1972: Wits is the first University to buy and operate a nuclear accelerator. The Tandem van de Graaff generator, called 'Daisy', is purchased for the Nuclear Physics Research Unit and pioneers the understanding of low-energy heavy-ion physics at just above the Coulomb barrier. Through the determined efforts of Professor Friedel Sellschop, an EN Tandem van de Graaff accelerator reaching 6 MV is obtained from the High Voltage Engineering Corporation and is installed in a purpose-designed building in 1973. In the same year, at a Senate meeting, the administration voices concern over the abbreviation 'Rand' cited on qualifications for academics and official publications from the University, which are increasingly confused with those of the new Rand Afrikaans University. Suggestions are made to change the citation to WWR, WU, UW, Wits, and R'RAND. The Senate settles on 'Wits' – which is the citation carried today on all academic credentials. On 8 June the second General Assembly is held, which affirms the rights of students to hold peaceful public assemblies.

1973: The Wits Law Clinic is established by Felicia Kentridge (who studied and worked at Wits in the 1960s) and opens in August. The clinic provides free legal advice by law students under the guidance of experienced members of staff. Kentridge is a pioneer of public interest law and the Wits Law Clinic gives much-needed support to impoverished Black South Africans. In its opening year, the clinic handles 145 cases, and in 1993 over 2 000 cases. A Wits student is banned due to a controversial cartoon that depicts Prime Minister John Vorster dumped down a toilet with a Wits student speaking down to him. This publication sparks calls from government ministers for the vice-chancellor at the time, Professor Guerino Bozzoli, to intervene.

1974: The Adler Museum of Medicine, founded by Drs Cyril and Esther Adler, is handed over to Wits. It is the only one of its kind in South Africa and is one of the most comprehensive medical history museums in the world. The first University library is renamed after William Cullen, who played a major part in the reconstruction of the building and its collection of books from around the world.

1975: Wits accommodates 10 600 students.

1976: The University expands into Braamfontein, and Senate House is completed to serve as the administration block of Wits.

1977: The All Sports Club officially opens and fills a need for a central clubhouse on campus. It is a venue for sports functions and a meeting place for athletes from within and beyond the University. Steve Biko, widely regarded as the founder of the Black Consciousness Movement in South Africa, dies in police custody on 12 September. Professor Phillip Tobias and other scholars write a formal complaint to the South African Medical Council about the treatment of Biko by the police. They also take the council to the Supreme Court regarding the matter. Senate House, the University's main administrative building, officially opens.

1978: The Centre for Applied Legal Studies (CALS), jointly funded by Wits and the Carnegie Corporation of New York, is established in 1978 to promote research into areas of the law affecting the Black community and civil rights. Wits Football secures the Mainstay Cup with a win over Kaiser Chiefs. As part of the new multiracial National Professional Soccer League, Wits Football becomes one of the first racially mixed teams to play in Black townships.

1979: The Standard Bank Foundation of Art is established, and it is agreed that a sum of money will be made available on an annual basis for the purchase of African art. The collection is owned by both Wits and Standard Bank. Today, the art collection is housed in the Wits Arts Museum. The Wedge, a building formerly owned by the National Institute of Metallurgy, is taken over by the University.

1980s

1981: Wits awards its 50 000th qualification.

1982: The Medical School moves to York Street in Parktown and the complex opens on 30 August. Sir Aaron Klug, a Wits alumnus, wins the Nobel Prize for Medicine.

1983: The Wits Theatre Complex opens its doors in July, ten years after the initial plan was announced. About R5 million is raised from the public and private sectors for the complex.

1984: Wits buys the Milner Park showgrounds from the Witwatersrand Agricultural Society and renames it the Braamfontein West Campus. The Wits Bridging Programme is officially launched across six faculties, following its establishment of part-time courses through the Centre for Continuing Education in the 1970s.

1985: Student numbers hover at around 16 400. On 16 August, the fifth Wits General Assembly reaffirms freedom, scholarship and service as the principles on which the University is based.

1987: A General Assembly responds to government's decision to impose conditions on the granting of university subsidies.

1988: Wits awards its 73 411th qualification.

1989: The Chamber of Mines Building for the Faculty of Engineering on the West Campus opens, and the 50-metre brick-paved AMIC deck is built across the M1 motorway to link the East and West campuses in Braamfontein.

1990s

1990: The Birth to Twenty programme, also known as 'Mandela's Children', is launched.

1991: Former Wits student Nadine Gordimer wins the Nobel Prize for Literature, seven years after Wits awarded her an honorary doctorate.

1992: The eighth Wits General Assembly calls on government to curb violence and combat poverty, and calls for a peaceful transition to democracy.

1993: Former South African president and Wits student Nelson Mandela wins the Nobel Peace Prize in recognition of his work for the peaceful termination of the apartheid regime, and for laying the foundations for a new democratic South Africa.

1994: The new South African democracy is born and, despite the touted concept of a rainbow nation, the nation remains on edge. Wits' campuses remain tense. In the same year, an organ built by the firm of Fehrle and Roeleveld, with tonal qualities said to follow the baroque and classical French traditions, is donated to Wits. It is housed in the Atrium in the South West Engineering Building on Braamfontein Campus East. The Atrium also serves as an occasional performance area for small music concerts arranged by the Wits School of Arts.

1996: Justice Richard Goldstone, a Wits alumnus, is appointed as the seventh chancellor of Wits University.

2000: A memorial sculpture is erected at the entrance to the Faculty of Health Sciences to commemorate the acceptance of the Internal Reconciliation Commission manifesto. The sculpture presents two interlocking figures. One looks down, representing the years of shame when students of colour were not allowed to participate fully in the training facilities at the Medical School because of the apartheid laws. The other figure is a student looking upwards and forwards towards the future, representing a united and non-racial Medical School.

2000s

2001: At a General Assembly held on 7 March, Wits launches its AIDS policy and confirms its commitment to fighting the epidemic. The Wits Institute for Social and Economic Research (WiSER), drawing on a history of advanced interdisciplinary research dating back to the 1960s, is established. Today, it shapes global and local thinking about political and cultural concerns of the post-colonial era.

2002: Wits alumnus Sir Sydney Brenner is awarded the Nobel Prize for Medicine. Six years later, he grants permission for Wits to name an institute in his name. Today, the Sydney Brenner Institute for Molecular Bioscience is a world-class multidisciplinary research institute dedicated to investigating the molecular and genomic aetiology of diseases among African populations. In the same year, the Wits Law Clinic successfully compels the government to provide nevirapine to HIV-positive mothers in a landmark case on mother-to-child-transmission, and fights for the provision of antiretroviral (ARV) treatment, which marks a turning point in the government's AIDS policy. The Wits Donald Gordon Hospital, South Africa's first and only private teaching hospital, officially opens. Sir Donald Gordon and his family donate R120 million to Wits to purchase the old Kenridge Hospital. Three years later, it partners with Mediclinic, and today it is a state-of-the-art specialist hospital that trains specialists and sub-specialists in South Africa.

2003: Professor Uwe Reimold, in an article published in *Science*, announces that there is massive evidence that bolides (meteors) are responsible for impact craters on Earth. A new 210- to 215-million-year-old dinosaur, named *Antetonitrus ingenipes* (the genus name, *Antetonitrus*, means 'before the thunder' and the species name, *ingenipes*, means 'massive feet'), is presented to the world by postdoctoral researcher Dr Adam Yates. Professor Phillip V Tobias hosts Dr Louis Leakey, who delivers the annual Orenstein Lecture in the Great Hall. International House, a residence designed for the growing international student population, is opened. The Student Union building is revamped and The Matrix mall opens.

2004: The Dalai Lama delivers a public lecture at Wits. He tries to return a few years later but is denied entry by the South African government. Wits students, staff and academics stage a protest against the government. Wits finds a pneumococcal vaccine that significantly reduces pneumonia in children. The new Wits Centre for Exercise Science and Sports Medicine opens in Parktown.

2005: Dr Mike Raath from the Wits Bernard Price Institute for Palaeontological Research identifies two 190-million-year-old dinosaur embryos, out of a group of seven eggs of an Early Jurassic prosauropod dinosaur, as the world's oldest dinosaur embryos. They are also the oldest known embryos of any terrestrial vertebrate from anywhere in the world. Wits hosts an Alumni General Assembly under the theme 'A Wits to Call Our Own', including a special graduation ceremony for those alumni who had conscientious reservations about the apartheid education system and therefore stayed away from their own graduation ceremonies. The Vice-Chancellor and Principal, Professor Loyiso Nongxa, apologises on behalf of the University and acknowledges the anger felt by many Black students who were at Wits during the apartheid years. The third annual African Presidential Roundtable takes place at Wits, attended by 12 former African heads of state, including Dr Kenneth Kaunda, Daniel arap Moi, Jerry Rawlings, Ali Hassan Mwinyi, General Abdulsalami Abubakar, Dr Navinchandra Ramgoolam, Dr Bakili Muluzi and Aristides Maria Pereira. The Department of Science and Technology (DST)/National Research Foundation (NRF) Centre of Excellence in Strong Materials based at Wits opens. The Wits node of the DST/NRF Centre of Excellence for Biomedical TB Research opens in May to advance TB research on the continent. The Joburg Centre for Software Engineering (JCSE) is opened to develop the growth of the local ICT sector and to serve as the nucleus for software development in Africa. The Marang Centre for Maths and Science Education opens under the leadership of Professor Mamokgethi Phakeng.

2006: Wits alumnus Rory Byrne, the chief constructor for Ferrari, receives an honorary doctorate. President Thabo Mbeki opens the Origins Centre on the Braamfontein Campus. The centre explores and celebrates the history of modern humankind and houses ancient stone tools, artefacts of symbolic and spiritual significance, and examples of the region's visually striking rock art. It captures the impact of the colonial era and highlights examples of resistance. It also boasts an extensive collection of rock art from the Rock Art Research Institute at Wits. Wits opthalmologist Dr Percy Amoils is awarded the Order of Mapungubwe Silver for his contribution to ophthalmology and for curing former president Nelson Mandela's 'chronic dry eyes'.

2007: Wits celebrates its 85th birthday. The University announces new clean, faster, cheaper fuel from coal research. The Emthonjeni Centre, a multidisciplinary centre that offers psychological, social work, speech pathology and audiology services to the public, opens. Deputy Chief Justice Dikgang Moseneke is installed as the eighth chancellor of Wits University. Wits bestows honorary doctorates on Johnny Clegg and Bruce Fordyce. Nobel Prize winner Amartya Sen delivers the Nadine Gordimer Lecture at Wits. The Centre for Indian Studies in Africa opens.

2008: The first Wits Arts and Literature Experience, hosted by the Faculty of Humanities, transforms the campus into a cultural epicentre. The first FIFA Medical Centre of Excellence in Africa opens at Wits. Wits alumnus and Nobel laureate Sir Sydney Brenner visits and signs an agreement allowing his name to be attached to the still-to-be-established Sydney Brenner Institute for Molecular Bioscience.

2009: Wits announces the discovery of a new species of dinosaur from the Early Jurassic period: *Aardonyx celestae*. A group of astronomers, including several Witsies, discover how the smooth disks of spiral galaxies are formed. A new species of mosquito is discovered. Wits researchers announce the discovery of the oldest fossilised human hair. The Wits Centre for Ethics opens.

2010s

2010: Professor Lee Berger and an international team announce *Australopithecus sediba*, a new species of hominid discovered by Mathew Berger, Lee's son, in 2008. Sir Richard Branson, Al Gore, President Jacob Zuma and other dignitaries view the fossils at Wits University. Wits physicists undertake research at the European Organization for Nuclear Research. Wits is acknowledged as the South African institution which produced the most scientific research publications pertaining to HIV/AIDS, between 1996 and 2000. Wits is accredited as a FIFA Medical Centre of Excellence, one of only six such centres in the world. Minister of Science and Technology Naledi Pandor opens the Palaeosciences Centre. The Wits Professional Development Hub, an R80 million building, opens its doors.

2011: A new student residence complex, the Wits Junction, and the Science Stadium on West Campus are opened. Professor Christopher Henshilwood and other researchers discover the world's oldest art studio – a 100 000-year-old ochre toolkit and workshop in the Blombos Cave at Still Bay. A novel technology to turn biomass (agricultural waste) and garbage (solid municipal waste) into liquid fuel, electricity, waxes and paraffin is announced and the BeauTi-FueL™ Project is displayed at COP17. The Centre for Applied Legal Studies wins a Constitutional Court case which declares the City of Johannesburg's housing policy unconstitutional and orders the City to provide temporary accommodation to evicted people. The Global Change and Sustainability Research Institute is launched.

2012: Wits is the custodian of some of the world's most priceless treasures and puts them on display during its 90th anniversary. They include the world's oldest dinosaur embryos; animal skeletons; human death masks; iron lungs used in South Africa during the 1950s poliomyelitis epidemic; seventeenth-century musical instruments; and Mandela's Rivonia Trial papers. The Centre for Applied Legal Studies wins a case that compels the state to deliver textbooks to all learners. The Shandukani Maternal and Child Health Centre in Hillbrow opens its doors. A memorial celebration is held to honour Professor Phillip Tobias after his death in June. Three Witsies are awarded prestigious National Orders: Professor Barry Schoub, Professor John Dugard and Dr Jonathan 'Johnny' Clegg. The Wits Mining Research Institute is launched.

2013: The School of Construction Economics and Management building opens in May. It completes the Built Environment Precinct along with the John Moffat Building extension and the Yale Telescope building. Wits joins a silent protest against rape and gender-based violence. The Centre of Excellence for the Palaeosciences opens, as does the Evolutionary Studies Institute. Wits hosts a memorial service in the Great Hall after the passing of former president Nelson Mandela in December. The new School of Public Health building opens in Parktown. Expeditions begin in the Rising Star cave system in the Cradle of Humankind World Heritage Site.

2014: Construction of the Nelson Mandela Children's Hospital begins on the Wits Education Campus in Parktown. Wits launches the Equality Scholarships and the Centre for Diversity Studies. A new Centre of Excellence in Mathematical and Statistical Sciences and the Centre for Excellence in Human Development are launched. The High-Throughput Electronics Laboratory opens.

2015: Wits students embark on a historic struggle for free, decolonised higher education in October. The #FeesMustFall protests quickly spread to other universities and around the country, culminating in a march to the Union Buildings. Wits is selected by the South African Medical Research Council to establish a new clinical cancer research centre. Professor Helen Rees receives the Harry Oppenheimer Fellowship Award. Professor Lee Berger announces the discovery of the largest fossil hominin find yet made in Africa: *Homo naledi*.

2016: #FeesMustFall protests continue and government makes concessions at the end of the year, which allow for access to education for more students. Senate House is renamed Solomon Mahlangu House, following a request from #FeesMustFall activists, in commemoration of the struggle stalwart. Wits agrees to insource thousands of workers. The Tshimologong Digital Innovation Precinct opens in Braamfontein. Setswana for 'new beginnings', Tshimologong is where the incubation of start-ups, the commercialisation of research, and the development of high-level digital skills for students, working professionals and unemployed youth take place. Four Witsies receive National Orders: Professor Benedict Wallet Vilakazi (posthumous); Professor Mamokgethi Phakeng, president of Wits Convocation; Professor Helen Rees, internationally renowned expert in HIV prevention, reproductive health and vaccines; and Wits alumnus and choreographer Sylvia 'Magogo' Glasser. Professor Lee Berger and Professor Glenda Gray make it to *Time* magazine's list of 100 most influential people in the world. Wits announces Africa's first chair in Digital Business.

2017: Central Block is renamed Robert Sobukwe Block to commemorate Sobukwe's service to the University and his contribution to fighting apartheid. Sobukwe, an intellectual of pan-Africanism and the founder and first president of the Pan Africanist Congress, is celebrated for his role in initiating and leading the anti-pass law protests of 21 March 1960. The Mathematical Sciences Building is renamed in honour of Dr Thamsanqa Wilkinson 'Wilkie' Kambule, an inspirational teacher and leader who fought for high-quality Black education. The Nelson Mandela Children's Hospital opens in Parktown. Wits physicists form part of an international observation of signals produced by the collision of two neutron stars. The Southern Centre for Inequality Studies opens, and Wits launches the eZone, a blended learning space to explore eLearning. The School of Animal, Plant and Environmental Sciences celebrates its 100th anniversary, having been established five years before the University was inaugurated.

2018: In a world-first, Wits doctors successfully transplant part of an HIV-positive mother's liver into her HIV-negative child in order to save the child's life. Three years later, the child remains HIV-negative. The Sibanye-Stillwater DigiMine opens at Wits. A new species of a giant dinosaur named *Ledumahadi mafube*, the largest land animal alive on Earth when it lived nearly 200 million years ago, is announced. Wits' Massive Open Online Courses (WitsX) introduces new courses on the EdX platform. The first-ever endocast reconstruction of the nearly complete 3.67-million-year-old brain of Little Foot reveals a small brain combining ape-like and human-like features.

2019: One hundred years after its establishment in 1919 as the Medical School, with just over 20 enrolled students, the Faculty of Health Sciences now includes seven schools with world-class research entities, and healthcare professionals and students who train and serve at a number of public and private hospitals and clinics in Gauteng province. Wits trains the highest number of specialists and sub-specialists in South Africa. 4IRSA (Fourth Industrial Revolution South Africa) is formed, of which Wits is a founding partner, and the first digital economy summit is opened by President Cyril Ramaphosa. Wits and Huawei launch the first 5G lab in Africa. Wits becomes the first IBM Q Network partner in Africa and enters into a collaboration with IBM to advance quantum computing on the continent. The Rock Art Engraving Archive opens at the Origins Centre. Professor Shabir Madhi receives the 2019 Harry Oppenheimer Fellowship Award. Wits calls for decisive action to be taken to end gender-based harm, xenophobia and Afrophobia on campuses and in society. The Wits rugby team beats defending champions North West University Puk 36–33 in the Pirates Grand Challenge final – its first tournament win since 1967. The Wits men's hockey team wins the 2019 University Sports of South Africa tournament, while the women's team is promoted to the A-division after winning the B-division.

2020s

2020: The COVID-19 pandemic strikes and Wits takes the academic programme online in three weeks. Wits Professor Shabir Madhi, the dean of the Faculty of Health Sciences, leads the first two Covid-19 vaccine trials. Wits students and staff create face shields for healthcare workers, pioneer new technologies to help people breathe more easily, and serve in hospitals, medical facilities, shelters and communities. Researchers at Wits create the world's first framework to better guide the management of terrestrial invasive species using big data. Two Wits academics play a leading role in writing and editing the Future Earth Report, published by the International Science Council, the UN and others. Jack Ginsberg donates an invaluable book arts collection to the Wits Art Museum.

2021: Professor Zeblon Vilakazi, a renowned nuclear physicist, takes the reins as vice-chancellor and principal on 1 January. Vilakazi also leads Cirrus, an academy-industry collaboration that seeks to advance artificial intelligence (AI) research and application capability in Africa. Wits forms an AI Africa Consortium to advance AI and to apply it in research and innovation. Wits and partners release an AI-powered algorithm to detect the third Covid-19 wave in South Africa. The Wits Quantum Initiative launches and provides a forum for quantum scientists to connect across all fields. Sixty years of human space travel is celebrated by the unveiling of a bust of Yuri Gagarin in the Planetarium at Wits. Professor Dilip Menon, director of the Centre for Indian Studies in Africa at Wits University, wins the prestigious international Falling Walls Award for his transnationalism research. Professor Roy Shires wins the International Excellence in Endocrinology Award, and Professor Paul Ruff is awarded the highest honour from the Cancer Association of South Africa. Two Witsies are awarded gold medals by the Academy of Science of South Africa: Professor Barry Schoub and Professor Shabir Madhi. Professor Saul Teukolsky, a Wits alumnus, is awarded the 2021 Dirac Medal and Prize by the International Centre for Theoretical Physics for his contribution to predicting the properties of gravitational waves that emerge from the collisions of black holes. Council passes the Wits Covid-19 Mandatory Vaccination Policy.

2022: Wits has five faculties (Commerce, Law and Management; Engineering and the Built Environment; Health Sciences; Humanities; and Science) and 33 schools, which offer approximately 3 400 courses to 38 000 students. Forty per cent of the student body comprises postgraduate students. Library facilities consist of two central libraries and 12 branch libraries with students having access to over 1.5 million books and journals. Approximately 6 000 students are accommodated in a number of residences and student villages. There are more than 30 sport clubs and about 75 student clubs and societies. Wits is also home to the Wits Theatre, the Origins Centre, the Planetarium, the Adler Museum of Medicine and a concert hall. The Chris Seabrooke Music Hall opens on 2 March. Shau Mafuna, a Wits mechanical engineer, joins the Mercedes AMG High-Performance Formula 1 team. Wits raises R2.1 billion of the R3 billion target for the Centenary Campaign, at the time of going to press.

NOTES

1 https://www.wits.ac.za/news/latest-news/general-news/2021/2021-01/our-moonshot-moment.html.

2 Sue Krige, *Wits: 90 Years of Making History* (Johannesburg: University of the Witwatersrand, 2011), 6.

3 Krige, *Wits*, 75.

4 Alan Paton, *Hofmeyr* (Oxford: Oxford University Press, 1964), 81.

5 Veronica Klipp, 'Honouring the "Father of Nguni Literature"', *The Heritage Portal Newsletter*, 28 April 2016, http://www.theheritageportal.co.za/article/honouring-father-nguni-literature.

6 *Mail & Guardian*, 'Warrior with a Pen', 18 August 2006, https://mg.co.za/article/2006-08-18-warrior-with-a-pen/.

7 Clement M Doke and Benedict W Vilakazi, eds., *Zulu-English Dictionary* (Johannesburg: Wits University Press, 1949).

8 Marc Augé, *Non-Places: An Introduction to Supermodernity* (London: Verso, 2009).

9 Kathy Munro, 'Wits Has Not Destroyed the Old Showground of Milner Park', *The Heritage Portal Newsletter*, 30 January 2020, http://www.theheritageportal.co.za/article/wits-has-not-destroyed-old-showground-milnerpark.

10 Phillip de Wet, 'The Closest Thing You Can Find to Wakanda in the Real World Is Wits, According to the World's Biggest News Agency', *Business Insider*, 22 March 2018, https://www.businessinsider.co.za/wits-is-the-place-closest-to-wakanda-2018-3.

11 Herbert Prins, 'The Nunnery at Wits', *The Heritage Portal Newsletter*, 5 November 2015, http://www.theheritageportal.co.za/article/nunnery-wits-created-weekend-and-still-going-strong.

12 The term 'umrabulo' has been in use for a good number of years, possibly gaining traction during the time of Robben Island political prisoners. It denotes political discussion or debate, sharing knowledge and education. It is also the title of a journal founded by the African National Congress in 1996.

13 Professor Adam Habib, former vice-chancellor and principal of Wits University, in his opening remarks at the launch of the upgraded WRC in Bushbuckridge, Mpumalanga, on 6 September 2019.

14 Professor Francois Engelbrecht, a lead author of the IPCC's *Special Report on Global Warming of 1.5°C (SR1.5)*, presentation on the physical basis of climate change during a 2019 outreach event of the IPCC 'Southern Africa Heading Towards Climate Tipping Points' in Accra, Ghana.

15 To hear more from these phenomenal women, listen to the *Wits Impacts for Good* podcast series, https://www.wits.ac.za/about-wits/wits-impacts-audio/.

16 Sisonke Study: https://www.samrc.ac.za/media-release/vast-majority-breakthrough-infections-vaccinated-health-workers-are-mild.

17 Read more at https://wits-vida.org.

18 Read more at www.wits.ac.za/covid19.

19 Read more at https://gp.coronavirus.co.za.

INTERVIEWEES

Lee Berger, Professor, Phillip V Tobias Chair in Palaeoanthropology and Head of the Centre for the Exploration of Deep Human History

Marcus Byrne, Professor, School of Animal, Plant and Environmental Sciences, Wits

Michele B. Chan, President, NantStudios

Julia Charlton, Senior Curator, Wits Art Museum

David Coplan, Emeritus Professor in Social Anthropology, Wits

Gillian Drennan, Professor and Head of School of Geosciences, Wits

Barry Dwolatzky, Emeritus Professor, former Head of Software Engineering, School of Electrical and Information Engineering, Wits and Head of the Joburg Centre for Software Engineering

Francois Engelbrecht, Distinguished Professor, Global Change Institute

Gabriella Farber, student, Wits SRC member

Andrew Forbes, Distinguished Professor, Structured Light Laboratory

Glenda Gray, Research Professor, Paediatrics, Wits School of Clinical Medicine and President and CEO, South African Medical Research Council

Fasiha Hassan, student leader, #FeesMustFall

Professor Kathleen Kahn, Co-founder, Medical Research Council/Wits Rural Public Health and Health Transitions Research Unit (Agincourt)

Thandeka Kathi, Attorney, Centre for Applied Legal Studies

Palesa Madi, Acting Deputy Director, Centre for Applied Legal Studies

Thuli Madonsela, Professor, Wits alumnus, former Public Protector and Chair in Social Justice, Stellenbosch University

Lesego Makinita, student, Wits SRC member

Musa Manzi, Professor and Director of Wits Seismic Research Centre

Stephen Matseoane, Emeritus Professor, Columbia University

Achille Mbembe, Research Professor in History and Politics, Wits

Bhekokuzakuye 'Keith' Mdlalose, Head of Protection Services, Wits

Bruce Mellado, Professor, Director of the Wits Institute for Collider Particle Physics and Senior Scientist at iThemba LABS

Mpendulo Mfeka, student, SRC President

Sphesihle Mndzebele, student, SRC member

Kathy Munro, Honorary Associate Professor, School of Architecture and Planning, Wits

Herbert Prins, former lecturer, Department of Architecture, Wits

Helen Rees, Professor and Executive Director, Wits Reproductive Health & HIV Institute

Bob Scholes, Distinguished Professor and Director, Global Change Institute

Mulala Simatele, Professor, Global Change Institute

Maurice Smithers, Director, Southern African Alcohol Policy Alliance in SA

Dr Patrick Soon-Shiong, Wits alumnus; CEO and Chair of NantWorks

Caroline Tiemessen, Research Professor, School of Pathology, Wits

Humphry Tlou, Co-ordinator, Maintenance and Operations, Institute for Collider Particle Physics

Stephen Tollman, Professor and Co-founder and Director of the Medical Research Council/Wits Rural Public Health and Health Transitions Research Unit (Agincourt)

Wayne Twine, Professor, School of Animal, Plant and Environmental Sciences, Wits and Head of Sustaining Natural Resources in African Ecosystems research programme

Zeblon Vilakazi, Professor and Vice-Chancellor and Principal of Wits

BIBLIOGRAPHY AND SOURCE MATERIAL

Augé, Marc. *Non-Places: An Introduction to Supermodernity*. London: Verso, 2009.

De Wet, Phillip. 'The Closest Thing You Can Find to Wakanda in the Real World Is Wits, According to the World's Biggest News Agency'. *Business Insider*, 22 March 2018. https://www.businessinsider.co.za/wits-is-the-place-closest-to-wakanda-2018-3.

Digby, Anne. http://www.samj.org.za/index.php/samj/article/viewFile/637/139%5C.

Doke, CM and BW Vilakazi. *Zulu-English Dictionary* (first edition). Johannesburg: Wits University Press, 1948.

Klipp, Veronica. 'Honouring the "Father of Nguni Literature"'. *The Heritage Portal Newsletter*, 28 April 2016. http://www.theheritageportal.co.za/article/honouring-father-nguni-literature.

Koopman, Adrian. 'Benedict Wallet Vilakazi: Poet in Exile'. *Natalia* 35 (2005): 63–74. https://www.natalia.org.za/Files/35/Natalia%2035%20pp63-74%20C.pdf.

Krige, Sue. *Wits: 90 Years of Making History*. Johannesburg: University of the Witwatersrand, 2011.

Mail & Guardian. 'Warrior with a Pen'. 18 August 2006. https://mg.co.za/article/2006-08-18-warrior-with-a-pen/.

Munro, Kathy. 'Wits Has Not Destroyed the Old Showground of Milner Park'. *The Heritage Portal Newsletter*, 30 January 2020. http://www.theheritageportal.co.za/article/wits-has-not-destroyed-old-showground-milner-park.

Ntshangase, Dumisane Krushchev. 'Between the Lion and the Devil: The Life and Works of B.W. Vilakazi 1906–1947'. University of the Witwatersrand, Institute for Advanced Social Research Seminar Paper No. 384, 21 August 1995. http://wiredspace.wits.ac.za/bitstream/handle/10539/9603/ISS-325.pdf?sequence=1&isAllowed=y.

Paton, Alan. *Hofmeyr*. Oxford: Oxford University Press, 1964.

Prins, Herbert. 'The Nunnery at Wits'. *The Heritage Portal Newsletter*, 5 November 2015. http://www.theheritageportal/article/nunnery-wits-created-weekend-and-still-going-strong.

Wits University. Alumni News, 18 July 2019. https://www.wits.ac.za/news/sources/alumni-news/2019/johnny-clegg-1953-2019.html.

Wits University. Archives, Alumni Relations. https://www.wits.ac.za/about-wits/history-and-heritage/. https://wits100.wits.ac.za/. https://www.wits.ac.za/alumni/history-and-traditions/history-of-wits/.

INDEX

A

activism at Wits 1, 23, 27–29, 31, 48, 50–51, 81, 87, 89, 193 *see also* apartheid, Wits mobilisation against/resistance to; #FeesMustFall movement
Adler, Cyril and Esther 73
Adler Museum of Medicine 73, 76–77, 196, 204
African Centre for Migration and Society (ACMS) 129
African National Congress (ANC) 24
African Research Universities Alliance (ARUA) 137
Aggett, Neil 27
Alexandra township 52, 100, 112
Andy Warhol exhibition, WAM 168, 171
apartheid 4, 21, 107–108, 151, 167
apartheid, Wits mobilisation against/resistance to 24–25, 27–31, 37, 90, 119, 173, 181, 194–195, 198
Archibald, Sally 101
artificial intelligence 3, 45, 108, 132, 134, 148, 161
Association of African Universities 137
Association of Commonwealth Universities 137
ATLAS detector 145–149
Attenborough, David 161
Augé, Marc 68
Australopithecus africana 57
Australopithecus sediba 24, 57, 60–61, 201

B

Ballim, Yunus 29
Bamford, Marian 60
Bank of America 171
Baragwanath Hospital (Bara) *see* Chris Hani Baragwanath Academic Hospital
Beadwork, Art and the Body exhibition, WAM 168
Berger, Lee 23, 57–58, 60–61, 201–202
Bernard Price Institute for Geophysical Research 20, 193
Bernard Price Institute for Palaeontological Research (BPI) 20, 23, 60, 200 *see also* Evolutionary Studies Institute
Birth to Twenty Programme, Soweto 95, 198
#BlackLivesMatter movement 48, 108
Black Students' Society (BSS) 28
Braamfontein 68, 77–78, 135, 171, 175, 182, 196, 201 *see also* Tshimologong Digital Innovation Precinct; Wits Art Museum
Braamfontein Campus East 12, 20, 23, 72, 195, 197–198
Braamfontein Campus West 17, 26, 73–75, 180, 197, 200

Brenner, Sydney 199, 201
Bristow, Tegan 135
Bronx Lebanon Hospital, New York 53
Buono, Wagner Tavares 138
Byrne, Marcus 160–163

C

Centre for Applied Legal Studies (CALS) 5, 47–51, 62, 197, 201 *see also* Wits Law Clinic
Centre of Excellence in Mineral and Energy Analysis 42
Centre of Excellence for the Palaeosciences 42, 55, 60, 201–202
Centre for the Exploration of the Deep Human Journey 57
Centre for Indian Studies in Africa 200, 204
Centre for Researching Education and Labour (REAL) 129
Chamber of Mines 14, 19, 23, 194, 197
Chan, Michelle B. 106–107
Charlotte Maxeke Johannesburg Academic Hospital 13, 107
Charlton, Julia 167–171
Chris Hani Baragwanath Academic Hospital 52–53, 113, 119, 136
Chris Seabrooke Music Hall 78–79, 171, 204
Clarke, Ronald 56–57
Clegg, Johnny 37–39, 196, 200–201
climate change deniers 161
climate change and sustainability endeavours, Wits 3, 43, 99, 101, 104–105, 201, 204 *see also* Global Change Institute
climate science excellence, Wits 99, 104–105
Cock, Richard 81
Coetzee, Hannelie 101, 182
Cohen, Nina 171
collaboration and partnership 51, 91, 96, 100–101, 104–105, 109, 171, 185, 203–204
collaborative networks 128–129, 131, 134, 136–137, 141, 146, 149
colonial modernism 70–71
Columbia University 53, 150
community development 90–91, 95–96
Conseil Européen pour la Recherche Nucléaire (CERN) programme *see* SA-CERN programme
contested spaces, Wits 70, 81 *see also* renaming of places and spaces
Coplan, David 37–39
coronavirus *see* Covid-19
Covid-19 48, 50–51, 68, 108, 115–116, 128, 204

211

Covid-19 Mandatory Vaccination Policy, Wits 204
Covid-19 Relief Fund, Wits 174
Covid-19 research/vaccine trials, Wits 4, 109–110, 112, 117, 124, 136–137, 147, 204
Cradle of Humankind World Heritage Site 23, 56–57, 61, 201

D

Dart, Raymond 23, 55, 57
decolonisation of higher education 4, 87, 201
Department of Anthropology 4, 28, 37–39, 169
Department of Architecture *see* School of Architecture and Planning
Department of Dramatic Art 78, 107
Department of Fine Arts 23, 71–72, 169
digital activism 50
digital arts *see* Wits Digital Arts Department
digital transformation 3–4, 68, 73, 126, 130, 134, 183, 185 *see also* eZones; Tshimologong Digital Innovation Precinct; Wits' Massive Open Online Courses
Dlamini, Judy 27
Dlamini, Mcebo 85
Doke, Clement M 26, 35–36, 193
Drennan, Gillian 41–45
Dugard, John 47, 201
dung beetles 161–163
Dwolatzky, Barry 155, 159

E

Empire Exhibition (1936) 68–69
Engelbrecht, Francois 99–100, 104–105
Evidence for Contraceptive Options and HIV Outcomes (ECHO) study 112
Evolutionary Studies Institute (ESI) 20, 55, 57, 60, 201
Extension of University Education Act (1959) 24–25, 194
eZones 126, 203

F

Faculty of Architecture 70–72
Faculty of Arts 192
Faculty of Commerce, Law and Management 12, 68, 204
Faculty of Engineering and the Built Environment 12, 23, 42, 68, 194, 197, 204
Faculty of Health Sciences 13, 22–23, 73, 109, 135–137, 192, 198, 203–204
Faculty of Humanities 12–13, 81, 201, 204
Faculty of Medicine *see* Faculty of Health Sciences
Fak'ugesi Festival 134–135, 158
Farber, Gabriella 185
Fassler, John 71–72, 81
#FeesMustFall movement 23, 48, 81, 84–89, 119, 196, 201

First, Ruth 28
First World War 18
food security endeavours, Wits 4, 43, 96, 104–105
Forbes, Andrew 139, 141–143
Future Earth 105, 204

G

5G laboratory, Wits 126, 131–132, 203
Garson, Fiona 171
Gauteng City-Region Observatory (GCRO) 77, 129–131
Gear, John 93
gender equality/justice 48, 50, 62–63, 131
Gender Research Project 62
Gender and Transformation Portfolio 175
gender-based violence 201, 206
geosciences *see* School of Geosciences
Ginsberg, Jack 170, 204
Giving Pledge 108
Global Change Institute (GCI) 99–101, 104–105, 201
Global South, Wits as intellectual hub of 4, 6, 51, 95–96, 104, 126, 128–129, 136, 151, 182–185 *see also* medical knowledge, Wits contribution to
Goldblatt, David 170
Goldstone, Richard 27, 198
Graduate School of Business *see* Wits Business School
Gray, Glenda 113, 117, 201
Gubbins collection of Africana 19

H

Habib, Adam 27, 97
Harlem Hospital, New York 53
Hassan, Fasiha 85, 87, 89
health innovation, Wits 107–109, 111–112, 117, 126, 135–136, 158, 199–200, 203
Heinke, Rex 174
Henshilwood, Christopher 57, 201
Higgs boson particle 145, 147
HIV research 113, 115, 199, 201, 203
HIV testing and treatment 110–112, 114 *see also* Wits Reproductive Health and HIV Institute
Hodgins, Robert 170
Hofmeyr, Jan H 16, 18, 21, 185, 192
Homo naledi 24, 61, 127, 201
Hood, Gavin 81
House Martienssen 71–72
House Munro 71
human rights, Wits promotion of 5, 47–51
Hutiri, Neo 158

I

IBM quantum computing initiative 4, 126–128, 133, 147, 153–155, 159, 185, 203
Ig Nobel Prize 160–161
inauguration, Wits (1922) 12, 15–18, 21, 185, 191
inclusivity/inclusion, narratives of 1, 3, 47–48, 50, 63, 109, 131, 147, 149, 182–183
inequality 1, 43, 58, 90, 102, 104, 125, 146, 177 *see also* Southern Centre for Inequality Studies
Intergovernmental Panel on Climate Change (IPCC) 99–100
Intergovernmental Platform on Biodiversity and Ecosystem Services 99
International Geosphere-Biosphere Programme 104
Internet of Things 4, 130
iThemba LABS 145–147, 149

J

Joburg Centre for Software Engineering (JCSE) 134, 155, 200
Johannesburg City Council 52, 73
Johannesburg, influence of Wits on 1, 3–4, 6, 12, 81, 181–182, 185 *see also* mining industry, intertwined histories of Wits and
John Moffat Building 70, 72, 81, 194, 201
Johnston, Claire 39
Juluka 38–39

K

Kahn, Kathleen 94–96
Kalla, Shaeera 85
Kathi, Thandeka 47–48
Kemp, Robert 119
Kennedy, Robert F 6, 195
Kentridge, William 81, 170
Khumalo, Cebolenkosi 173
Khumalo, Mzilikazi 81
Kimberley 13, 15, 192

L

LA Times 107–109
Large Hadron Collider 145, 184
Lawson, Wilfred 23, 77–78
Le Corbusier 71
legacy of Wits 42, 81, 89
LGBTQIA+ community 169, 175
Little Foot 56–57, 61, 203
Los Angeles 107–109

M

Madhi, Shabir 109, 112, 136–137, 203–204
Madi, Palesa 48–51
Madonsela, Thuli 62–63
Makapansgat, Limpopo 23, 195
MakerSpace 133, 152
Makinita, Lesego 175
Makutu, Mpho 133, 152
Malahlela-Xakana, Mary Susan 26, 193
Mandela, Nelson 31, 34, 193, 198, 200–201
Manzi, Musa 42–43
Martienssen, Heather 71
Martienssen, Rex 70–72
Matseoane, Stephen 52–53
Mbembe, Achille 150–151
Mchunu, Sipho 38
Mdlalose, Bhekokuzakuye 'Keith' 118–121
medical knowledge, Wits contribution to *see* health innovation, Wits
Medical School 22–23, 52, 73, 113, 193, 195, 197–198, 203 *see also* Faculty of Health Sciences
Meer, Fatima 81
Mellado, Bruce 145–147, 149
Merrill Lynch SA 176
Mfeka, Mpendulo 172
migrants/migrant populations 129, 181, 195
Milner, Lord Alfred 21, 68
Milner Park 12, 15, 21, 23, 68, 192, 197 *see also* Rand showgrounds
miners' protest (1899) 180
miners' strike (1922) 16–18, 21
mining industry, intertwined histories of Wits and 1, 4, 12–15, 18, 21, 31, 41, 50, 180, 197 *see also* South African School of Mines and Technology
Mkhatshwa, Nompendulo 85
Mnama, Yonela 171
Mndzebele, Sphesihle 172
Morris, Lynn 115, 117
Moseneke, Dikgang 27, 200
Muholi, Zanele 169
Munro, Kathy 69
Musk, Elon 45

N

NantWorks 106–108
National Party government 21, 24, 193
National Research Foundation 55, 115, 128, 146–147
National Union of South African Students (NUSAS) 31
Nelson Mandela Children's Hospital, Parktown 202–203
Nkadimeng, Edward 146, 149
Nobel Prize winners 26, 57, 197–201
Nongxa, Loyiso 27, 29, 200
non-racialism 28, 31, 195, 198 *see also* open university, Wits as
Nqebelele, Nolubabalo Unati 27

Nuclear Physics Research Unit 195–196

O
open university, Wits as 6, 24–26
Oppenheimer, Ernest 22, 195
Oppenheimer, Harry 115, 194, 202–203
Oppenheimer Life Sciences Building 6
Order of Ikhamanga 36, 39
Origins Centre 23, 57, 200, 203–204

P
palaeoanthropology 4, 57, 60–61
palaeontology *see* Bernard Price Institute for Palaeontological Research
palaeosciences 57, 60 *see also* Centre of Excellence for the Palaeosciences
pan-Africanism 91, 203
Parktown Campus 12–13, 22–23, 73, 77, 195, 197, 199, 202 *see also* Savernake
Pearce, Geoffrey 69
Pelebox 158
Pereira, Laura 104
Phillip V Tobias Fossil Primate and Hominid Laboratory 55–56
Phillips, James 81
Phillips, Lionel 19
Planetarium 73, 163, 195, 204 *see also* Wits Digital Dome
Posel, Deborah 128
power relations, reimagining/challenging of 47, 51, 130
Preller, Alexis 68
Price, Bernard 18, 20, 60, 193
Protection Services, Wits 118–119, 121
public good, Wits' advancement of 1, 3, 81, 169, 181, 185

R
racial discrimination/colour bar 21, 35–36, 63, 175
racial segregation, ideology of 26
Radebe, Xolani 135
Rand Easter Show *see* Rand showgrounds
Rand Rebellion (1922) 16
Rand showgrounds 12, 68–70, 197
Randlords 15, 18–19
Rees, Helen 111–112, 117, 202
reflection seismology technology 42–43
renaming of places and spaces 16, 23–24, 81–82, 192, 196–197, 202–203
Rhodes, Cecil John 16, 19
Rhodes University 24, 194
#RhodesMustFall campaign 89
Rising Star cave system 24, 61, 202
Robotics, Autonomous Intelligence and Learning Lab, Wits 132

Rodriguez-Fajardo, Valeria 142
Rubidge, Bruce 55, 57

S
SA-CERN programme 137, 145–147, 149
Savernake 18–20, 195
Scholes, Bob 100–101, 104, 105
School of Animal, Plant and Environmental Sciences 96, 160, 203
School of Architecture and Planning 69, 72, 91 *see also* Faculty of Architecture
School of Computer Science and Applied Mathematics 132, 159
School of Electrical and Information Engineering 4, 128, 134
School of Geosciences 41–42, 45
School of Medicine *see* Medical School
School of Mines *see* South African School of Mines and Technology
School of Mining Engineering 21, 42, 45
School of Physics 139, 145–146, 149
School of Public Health 95, 202
Schoub, Barry 201, 204
scientific innovation, Wits' international footprint 141–142, 145, 147, 149, 184–185, 204
Scilinx 132
Second World War 21–22, 36, 70, 72, 193
Seismic Research Centre 42–43
Sekoto, Gerard 168–169
Senate House 23, 81, 87, 196–197, 202
Sharpeville massacre 70
Singh, Keshaan 138
Skotnes, Pippa 170
Smithers, Maurice 28, 90–91
Smuts, Jan 16, 18, 21
social justice, Wits commitment to 3, 5, 47, 51, 62, 77, 81, 91, 130, 183
social transformation, Wits commitment to 24, 89, 125–126, 129, 149 *see also* digital transformation
Solomon Mahlangu House 23, 81, 87, 196, 202
Soon-Shiong, Patrick 106–109
South African Medical Research Council 94, 113, 115, 137, 202
South African School of Mines and Technology 15–16, 18, 192
Southern Centre for Inequality Studies 36, 130, 203
spatial development of Wits 12, 19–22
Square Kilometre Array (SKA) project 147, 149
Standard Bank African Art Collection 169, 197
Stegmann family 23, 195
Stellenbosch University 63
Sterkfontein farm 23, 56–58, 61, 194
Stern, Irma 68, 169

Structured Light Laboratory, Wits 138–139, 141–143
Student Union 195, 199
Students' Moderate Alliance (SMA) 31
Students' Representative Council (SRC) 20, 81, 85, 87, 172–175, 193, 195–196
Sustaining Natural Resources in African Ecosystems (SUNRAE) 96–97
Swartkrans farm 23, 195

T
Tan, Ling 135
Tandem van de Graaff accelerator 23, 195
Taung child, skull of 54–55
The Digital Imaginaries: Premonition exhibition 135
The Nunnery Theatre 79–81, 107
The Wedge 23, 197
Thibela, Thakgalo 27
Tiemessen, Caroline 113, 115, 117
Tintswalo Hospital 94–95
Tlou, Humphrey 146
Tobias, Phillip V 13, 23, 29, 57, 196, 199, 201
Tollman, Stephen 94–97
Tower of Light 12, 69–70, 74
Transvaal Technical Institute 16, 192
Tshimologong Digital Innovation Precinct 68, 125, 131–134, 153–155, 157, 159, 202 *see also* Fak'ugesi Festival
Tutu, Desmond 34, 193
Twine, Wayne 97
Tyson, Peter 104

U
Unisa 26, 34
United Democratic Front (UDF) 28
University of Cape Town 24, 89, 194 *see also* #RhodesMustFall campaign
University Corner, Braamfontein 23, 77–78
University of Johannesburg 48, 129
University of Natal 24, 193
University of the Western Cape 24
urbanisation/urban related research 93, 100, 104, 181–182

V
Verwoerd, Hendrik 70
Vilakazi, Benedict Wallet 26, 33–36, 180, 193, 202
Vilakazi, Khulani 33
Vilakazi, Zeblon Zenzele 4, 6, 27, 147, 154, 156, 184–185, 204
vision/core purpose of Wits 3, 6, 182–184
Vogel, Coleen 101, 104–105

W
Wald, Herman 194–195

Walter Battiss collection, WAM 168
water security/management 43, 104–105
Webster, David 28, 30, 39
William Cullen Library 19, 196
Williams, Lesley Donna 159
Wits Art Museum (WAM) 77–79, 166–171, 197, 204
Wits Business School 13, 22, 195
Wits Centre for Diversity Studies 130, 202
Wits Cultural Precinct 81
Wits DigiMine 36, 42, 203
Wits Digital Arts Department 79, 134, 158, 171
Wits Digital Dome 73, 163
Wits Donald Gordon Medical Centre 136, 199
Wits Drama programme *see* Department of Dramatic Art
Wits Earth Sciences cluster 41
Wits Education Campus (WEC) 13 *see also* Wits School of Education
Wits Education Policy Unit (EPU) 129
Wits Food Bank 175
Wits for Good manifesto 6
Wits Great Hall 1, 5, 20, 81, 119, 173, 193–194, 199, 202
Wits Institute for Social and Economic Research (WiSER) 128, 151, 198
Wits Isotope Geosciences Laboratory (WIGL) 41–42
Wits Journalism 77
Wits Law Clinic 47, 196, 199
Wits' Massive Open Online Courses (WitsX) 126, 203
Wits Mining Institute 42, 201
Wits Music 134
Wits Perinatal HIV Research Unit (PHRU) 113
Wits Reproductive Health and HIV Institute (Wits RHI) 111–112, 116
Wits Rural Campus (WRC), Mpumalanga 12, 93–95, 135, 183
Wits Rural Knowledge Hub 97
Wits Rural Public Health and Health Transitions Research Unit (a.k.a. Agincourt) 94–95, 136
Wits School of Arts 77–79, 81, 135, 171, 198
Wits School of Clinical Medicine 113
Wits School of Education 13, 129
Wits Theatre Complex 81, 171, 197, 204
Wits University Press (WUP) 35, 77, 91, 192
Witwatersrand Agricultural Society 12, 19, 68, 70, 197
Working on Fire project 102–103
World Health Organization 95, 112, 117

XYZ
xenophobia, Wits action against 29, 181, 203
Yeoville, Johannesburg 90–91
Yeoville-Bellevue Community Development Trust 91
Zaidel-Rudolph, Jeanne 81
Zulu language 33–36, 192, 202

Published in South Africa by:
Wits University Press
1 Jan Smuts Avenue
Johannesburg 2001

www.witspress.co.za

© University of the Witwatersrand, Johannesburg 2022
Photographs © Copyright holders

First published 2022

978-1-77614-735-9 (Paperback)
978-1-77614-736-6 (Hardback)
978-1-77614-737-3 (Web PDF)
978-1-77614-738-0 (EPUB)

All rights reserved. No part of this publication may be reproduced, stored in a retrieval system, or transmitted in any form or by any means, electronic, mechanical, photocopying, recording or otherwise, without the written permission of the publisher, except in accordance with the provisions of the Copyright Act, Act 98 of 1978.

All images remain the property of the copyright holders. The publishers gratefully acknowledge the publishers, institutions and individuals referenced in captions for the use of images. Every effort has been made to locate the original copyright holders of the images reproduced here; please contact Wits University Press in case of any omissions or errors.

This book is freely available under a CC-BY-NC-ND 4.0 Creative Commons License. (https://creativecommons.org/licenses/by-nc-nd/4.0/).

Centenary project management: Wits Advancement Division
Authors: Wits Communications and Roth Communications
Additional photo research: Shivan Parusnath
Project manager: Inga Norenius
Cover artwork: Jignasa Diar
Cover design and layout: Hybrid Creative

www.ingramcontent.com/pod-product-compliance
Lightning Source LLC
Chambersburg PA
CBHW081708100526
44590CB00022B/3697